Praise for *The Ames Farm of Wool*

It was a very different time, and I want to tell the story about what it was like then, before it is forgotten.

In her memoir, Roberta Ames tells of the family farm at its best—houses and sheds and barns in a landscape of rivers and fields, meadows and woodlots; the glorious interdependence between animals and the people who cared for them; the vital reciprocity within an agricultural community—a way of life long gone.

This book is the real deal.

—Deborah Gould, author of
The Eastern: The Early Years and *The Eastern: Later On*

Roberta Ames's engaging memoir is a vivid account of the rural Maine experience from the Great Depression to the years after World War II. Growing up on an ancestral farm in Woolwich, she learned of the hard work and self-reliance required to live on the land. In this clearly written and handsomely produced book, Roberta tells a story both personal and universal. It is a valuable record of a time now passed.

—Earle G. Shettleworth, Jr., Maine State Historian

This is a remarkable and vivid recollection of life on a Maine farm in the 1930s and '40s, lovingly and proudly shared. A thorough and useful source, and a special trip down memory lane for those of us who also grew up in that first half of the 20th century.

—Alan Baker, former long-time publisher of
the *Ellsworth American* and the *Mount Desert Islander*

This wonderful reminiscence, rich with detail, concerns life on a small Maine dairy farm of the mid-1900s, one of many thousands of which would not survive as a sustainable economic entity beyond the next generation or two. The children of these vanished farms, however, such as the author, early experienced a traditional way of life which would remain embedded within them throughout their lives.

—W. H. Bunting, author of *A Day's Work*,
The Camera's Coast, *Sea Struck*, *Live Yankees*, and more

The Ames Farm
of
Woolwich, Maine

―――⇒➤●◄⇐―――

Life of an American Family

―――⇒➤●◄⇐―――

A Memoir by Roberta Ames
as told to Erik Lund

Cover and book design by Lindy Gifford

Editing by Genie Dailey

Cover photograph and on page 97 by Tom Jones
Map by Rhumb Line Maps and Lindy Gifford
All family snapshots from the author's collection
All current photographs of the author and the property by Erik Lund

*I once told my Dad that I wouldn't have been raised
by any other people in any other place.*

—Roberta Ames

Contents

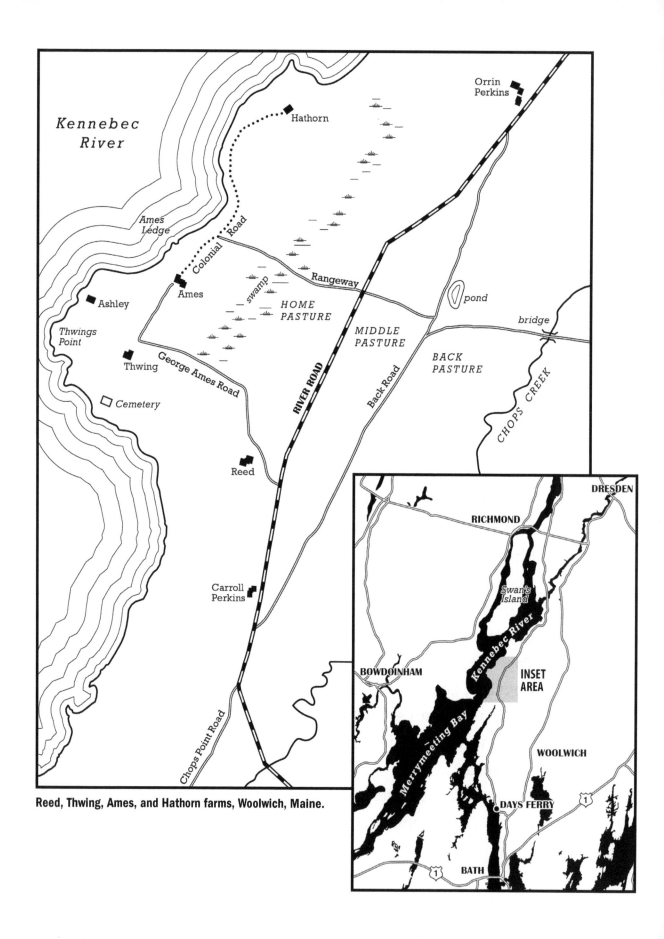

Reed, Thwing, Ames, and Hathorn farms, Woolwich, Maine.

Foreword

The Ames Farm is 100 acres of fields and woods located in an area significant in American history, on the east side of the Kennebec River in Woolwich, Maine. Woolwich itself is across the river from one of the great 19th- and 20th-century industrial centers of Maine, the shipbuilding City of Bath. The area was the subject of Massachusetts-based land speculation in the middle of the 18th century, when ownership of land in Maine was nebulous and contested among Native Americans, the beneficiaries of land grants from the King of England, and the beneficiaries of land grants from the Province of Massachusetts, of which Maine was then a part.

The author's great-great-great grandfather, Jacob Eames, purchased his title to the land from one of those speculators, the Clarke & Lake Company, in 1779. (An account of the Farm's acquisition and the land disputes surrounding it—which is itself of historical interest—can be found in this book's Afterword.) Jacob Eames was the first to build a home on the land and to farm it.

The Farm is located on the Kennebec River just north of Merrymeeting Bay, the great confluence of six rivers melding into the lower Kennebec above the Chops, a 600-foot-wide waterfall that is drowned by every incoming tide. Well before the Eames purchase, the site of the first European settlement in the area—then part of the frontier—was on a point of land now called Thwings Point abutting the Farm and jutting into the river.

There, Thomas Ashley, a fur trader and tavern keeper, had built a home, tavern, and trading post more than a century before Jacob Eames's purchase. Ashley had probably come to New England as an indentured servant in the Puritan migration, and had come north to the frontier when his servitude ended (www.wikitree.com). His home and tavern was a gathering place for the settlers in the area. In 1654, a group of settlers met at Ashley's home on Thwings Point to form the first Colonial government in the Merrymeeting Bay region.

In September 1775, four years before Eames's purchase, Benedict Arnold, at the direction of General George Washington, had led a force of 1100 Continental Army troops across this land on their way north to an unsuccessful attempt to capture the City of Quebec. They had crossed the river south of the Farm at what was then the only Kennebec River crossing from Bath, to Days Ferry in Woolwich, and had camped on Swan Island in the river. Swan, between the towns of Richmond and Dresden, is just north of what became the Ames Farm and is easily seen from there.

Arnold and his troops also stopped at the Pownalborough Courthouse in Dresden, built fourteen years earlier. John Adams had successfully represented a client there in 1765 and must have followed the same route, on horseback, as the only other travel option was by riverboat up the Kennebec, an opportunity Adams's journal makes clear he declined.

The Farm was at the center of the ice trade in the 1800s, when pure Kennebec River ice, prized everywhere, even in India, was harvested from the river and stored in great icehouses along the river until the river thawed in the spring. Then the ice blocks could be loaded onto sailing vessels for shipment to cities along the East Coast and south around Cape Horn on the way to Asia. The three largest icehouses on the Kennebec, owned by the Morse Ice Company of Bath, were located at Thwings Point, the Farm's southern neighbor. Farmers all along the Kennebec worked in the ice trade in winter, including some named Ames. Some others were also housed at the Ames Farm.

This memoir by Roberta Ames describes the subsistence farming life of her family in a sliver of time, the 1930s through the 1950s. They were the last members of the Ames family to live on and work the land their family had owned since 1779.

I had the good fortune to buy the Farm in 1995, after it had passed through the Ames family's ownership and that of two other owners. Roberta and I became friends then; she told me about the history of the Farm, and she loaned me her mother's diaries and photos, some of which appear throughout this book. Our collaboration didn't result in a book then, but now it has, twenty-six years later, and we are both pleased.

Erik Lund
Ames Farm
Woolwich, Maine
June 2021

Introduction

Hello, I'm Roberta Ames.

I was born in 1931 and grew up on my family's farm—the Ames Farm—in Woolwich, across the Kennebec River from Bowdoinham. Five generations of my Ames family farmed there, starting with my great-great-great grandfather, Jacob Eames, who bought the land—100 acres—in 1779.

I grew up without electricity because Central Maine Power Company made you pay for their poles if you wanted electricity, and we couldn't afford it. We were just trying to survive the Depression.

Ours was a dairy farm. We had fifteen milk cows that we had to milk every morning at 4:30 a.m. and again in late afternoon for the dairy, and another ten calves and heifers we were raising. And the bull.

We didn't have running water. We had dug wells, two of them, and had to pump the water by hand until we got a gas-driven pump to help.

The cattle had to be fed and watered and so did our two horses and the pig and the chickens.

We didn't buy food at the supermarket. We raised our food, or hunted it.

We didn't have a refrigerator. We had an icebox and an icehouse where we stored the ice we'd cut by hand from the river in winter and the horses had hauled.

My Mom ran the household, without any help besides our family.

We survived, but farming was hard, just like it had been for generations of Ameses before us, and the 1930s were a lean time. There were a lot of things we didn't have, but what we did have, like other Ameses had had, were family, friends, and neighbors.

There wasn't a whole lot of money around, and farmers needed to work together and share. Chickens will lay eggs without a rooster, but if you want fertilized eggs and chicks, you borrowed someone's rooster for a week. In winter, when ice was being cut for icehouses, everyone pitched in and my Dad would supply his ice groover and team of horses; in spring, when it was time to plow, a neighbor would bring down his manure spreader, help us shovel the manure out of the barn cellar and spread it on the fields; haying and filling the barns for the winter was a community event; in the fall, when dried logs were being cut into stove wood, a portable gas-powered saw made the rounds from farm to farm.

I had four siblings, one a sister sixteen years older than me, and three boys in between us. I was the youngest by seven and a half years. When World War II happened, my sister was married, and two of my three brothers joined the Air Force (one served as a tail gunner in a B-17). After the war, times were good. My brothers found good-paying jobs, and none of them wanted to come back to take over the farm.

When I graduated high school, I decided to stay on—my Dad, George Ames, had no one else in the family to work the farm with him—and when I married, my husband Victor and I moved into the house and helped my Dad and my Mom with all the work the farm needed. Our help wasn't enough.

In the end, my Dad had to sell his herd of cattle and sell the land to which the Ames family had been attached for nearly 200 years. Times had changed, everything around us had changed, and we could no longer manage to keep it up.

It was a very different time, and I want to tell the story about what it was like then, before it is forgotten.

CHAPTER ONE

George Ames Road

The Ames Farm, where I was raised, is six miles upriver from Days Ferry and six-tenths of a mile downhill from the Reed house on a gravel road off the River Road. Our road first passes the Reed house, then heads off downhill, turns left at the bottom of the hill heading toward the river and crosses a bog on its way toward the Thwings' house. The Thwings' house is on a hill up to the left of the road, and just below it, the road takes a right-angle turn north around what was once the Thwings' barn (long gone now) over to my family's farmhouse. We were across the river from Bowdoinham, three-quarters of a mile away. Merrymeeting Bay was south of us.

Before the Carlton Bridge was built in the 1920s, people going between Bath and Wiscasset had to cross the Kennebec River by ferry. One of the ferries ran from north of Bath across to Days Ferry. The old Stage Road to Wiscasset went from the top of the Days Ferry landing.

Ferry landing at Days Ferry ca. 1890, showing the beginning of the old road to Wiscasset.
Picture postcard from the author's collection.

The part of the road from Thwing's to our place was laid out in Colonial times and is referred to in the 1779 deed to my great-great-great grandfather, Jacob Eames (Appendix A). It keeps on beyond our place, following the river north to the Hathorn farmhouse, which is just a cellar hole now.

When Jacob Eames took his deed, there were four farms side by side, Reed, Thwing, Eames, and Hathorn. All four of those families have headstones in the small cemetery on the other side of Thwing's.

The Hathorn land was acquired by my mother's mother and her second husband in the 1930s, and they built a cottage there, not far from the riverbank. A lot of that area is woods now, but when I was growing up, it was fields and pasture. My Dad used to grow a cash crop of vegetables there, keep it in hay for my grandmother and her husband, and harvest the hay every year. He also supplied them with ice from our ice stack.

South of us toward Days Ferry, people who weren't farmers owned fields they wanted hayed; Dad cut their fields in exchange for the hay.

When my grandmother died (after surviving her husband and marrying a third time), she left the land to my Mom, and the Hathorn farm was added to ours. Even with the Hathorn land, Dad couldn't raise enough hay to keep our herd in feed through the winter and had to cut hay elsewhere to have enough.

There wasn't much of a road between us and the Thwings before the Depression, just a gravel track, because the River Road that's now just east of us hadn't been built yet, and each of the three farms had its own driveway to a main road that was considerably further to the east. That road had a stone bridge over the Chops Cross Creek that connected to Chops Cross Road, which came back down toward the river and the River Road, then back over to Days Ferry.

One of the Feds' Depression-era projects was to extend the River Road from that junction down a steep gully, across a new bridge, and uphill again past the Reed house and straight across our farm. The new River Road cut off the top third of our farm from the lower two-thirds. That top third had been part of our pasture land. We were still able to use it, but it was a lot harder because we had to cross the River Road, which was now the main road for traffic.

Once the River Road extension had been built, it made sense to connect the three farms (the Hathorn farm was vacant by then) by a single road to the River Road, and that's what was done. My Dad was Woolwich's Road Commissioner, and he built the road, with my brothers' help.

The straight stretch of George Ames Road heading toward Thwing's.

The land between us and Thwing's was pretty low and wet and required a lot of gravel fill. The Reed house sat on a hill of gravel, and a lot of the gravel came from there. Mom's diary has a lot of entries about my Dad and my brother George "going for gravel." That's where they were going, and that's what it was for.

The piece of the road from the River Road past the Reed house was downhill on that hill of gravel to where it connected to the section that used to be the Thwings' rangeway. From there, it was a straight shot across the bog culverts to the corner by the Thwings' barn.

All this happened when I was too young to remember it. The older road was still there when I was growing up, and we called it the "back road." People still used it, so long as the stone bridge was up, but the road wasn't kept up. You can find it, if you look, but the stone bridge is in pieces.

The town called the road Dad built "George Ames Road," and that's what it was for sixty years, including all the years I lived there.

Sometime in the 1960s, the Thwing house, which had been vacant for a long time, was bought by John and Jeanette Cakouros. John was (or would become) a well-liked schoolteacher in Woolwich and Bath. Both Dad and Mom met and liked him. Jeanette was also a teacher, and considered herself a student of history. Some decades after Dad had sold the farm, she decided that the name of the road should reflect the fact that its first stop after Reed's—Thwings Point, where her house was—should be the name of the road, because Thwings Point had been the site of the first Colonial government building in the area (centuries long gone now, with almost no trace) and because she was living in the Thwing house.

I can understand that. We'd been gone from the farm for thirty years by then. My Dad's name on the road only reflected who had built it. But no one asked me or my brother George (who lived in Bath) what we thought about it. I didn't like it, and I'm sad about it.

The road Dad built, which leads to our farmhouse, is now called Thwings Point Road.

———➤●⊰———

CHAPTER TWO

George M. Ames

My Dad, George Ames, was born on April 8, 1892, in the Ames farmhouse to David and Blanch (Howe) Ames. He had a sister, Annie, four years older, but no other siblings. His father died suddenly, and tragically, when Dad was 12, by drowning in the river alongside the farm.

Annie married David Henderson (who was raised in Nova Scotia) in 1909, and the two of them ran Henderson's Dairy Farm in Bath. They were lifelong friends with my Dad and Mom. The Bath golf course came from their land.

Dad quit school and went to work in the woods, cutting and selling wood to help support my grandmother and the farm. They had a horse that he took in the woods with him. They only had a couple of cows to supply them with milk. Not sure what they used for money, but they managed.

When he was old enough to sign on, he went to work at the Hyde Windlass Company (which became part of Bath Iron Works later on).

He must have learned how to be a mechanic while at Hyde. He was a good mechanic, even though he had no formal training. I think his talent was instinctive. When I was quite young, he built a tractor out of a Ford coupe chassis. The seat was from a hay rake, and there was a block of granite to give it weight. It was a great machine, and we used it for the life of the farm.

The Hyde Windlass Company built ship's machinery, including windlasses, capstans, and steering gear, some steam-powered and some human-powered. Hyde Windlass was the ancestral company of today's Bath Iron Works. They sent their machinery all over the world.

While he was working at Hyde, Ed Jaquith introduced him to my Mom, who played the organ at the church she attended in Bath, where she grew up. She was probably 18 or 19. They hit it off, and were married in 1913, on his 21st birthday. First off, he brought her to the farm to live with his widowed mother.

Then, because he was a good mechanic, he got a job at the Maine State Garage in Skowhegan, and they lived there for a couple of years.

When Mom became pregnant, they moved back to the farm in 1915, where my sister Ruth was born. My brother Harold was born there in 1916. Not sure what my father did to earn money in those years, either, but my brother Gilbert was born there in 1921 and my brother George in 1924.

Meantime, he was buying cows and building the herd for what became our dairy farm.

My Dad was not a big man, about five foot six and a hundred forty pounds, but he never seemed to get tired. He was up at 4:30 a.m. every morning to do chores and milk the cows; he pumped water for them (and for us); he took them out to pasture; he tended the horses, including pumping water for them, shoeing them twice a year for winter or spring, seeing to it they were warm; in winter, he went out and cut the wood we needed to heat the house and the woodstoves; he built and he shingled; he cut and he welded metal to repair farm equipment; he cut river ice and stored it in the ice stack; in warmer weather, he cut the

George Ames in the field in front of our house.

stored ice into chunks he would put into the iceboxes, both ours and my grandmother's; and every day, summer or winter, he had to see to the chores, getting the milk into the cooler in the milk house, where we had to keep the water below is 36° before we could then take the milk cans out of the cooler for delivery to the dairy.

Dad would never buy anything he couldn't pay for, then and there, and, for whatever reason, he carried all the money he had in his wallet in his back pocket. One day after he had been plowing, the wallet was gone. He knew it had worked out of his pocket while plowing but not sure where, of course. He and neighbors and family searched for two days, turning over the clods where he'd last plowed, trying to find it with no success. It was never found.

You don't recover from that kind of loss when that's all you have. He didn't like to owe money, and he didn't like to take help from people, but then he had no choice. We only got paid for milk every two weeks. My brothers and sister—they were grown and out of the farm—helped as much as they could, but it was a real hard time. He left his wallet inside the house after that. Also didn't keep all his money in his wallet.

In the 1940s, he ran for and was elected as Woolwich Road Commissioner. The position was unpaid, but he could bill the town for hours worked, including responding to or investigating a road-related problem. There were a lot of those hours. My brother George was the only one that helped him when he was road commissioner.

Dad used to say that if no one can find a bad thing to say about a person when they die, it means they lived a good life. That was descriptive of him. He was kind to people and animals. He was extremely thoughtful, putting others first.

Dad was a good father. It must have been difficult to have three boys and two girls to teach along with all of the work there was to do. As busy as he was, he always found time to help when it was needed. He used to say he never got tired, and I would think, what is wrong with him? Only after I was working two or three jobs at a time did I understand what he meant. The secret is loving what you do.

He loved music and was a very good dancer. We grew up on the dance floor. There was a building in Days Ferry where they had dances on Saturday nights. He used to take everybody, and if I got tired, I went to sleep on the benches. There were no babysitters in those days, so wherever he and Mom went, everyone had to go.

He tried not to do major work on Sundays, but if we had a lot of rain, work had to be done whenever there was sunshine.

He listened to the news when he had time. One of those times was in the morning when he was shaving. When Pearl Harbor was bombed, he had the news on and was listening while it was actually happening. Not long after, Gilbert and George enlisted in the Air Force. They both wanted to be pilots, they enlisted on the same day, and they left home on the same day to serve our country. That was one of the two times I saw my Dad cry. We didn't know if we'd ever see them again.

Dad shaved with a straight razor, which fascinated me, so I asked if he minded if I watched while he shaved. He said that was okay, so I used to watch him shaving sometimes.

Gil did become a pilot, but wasn't stationed overseas. George failed the pilot's eye exam and became a tail gunner on a B-17. He couldn't tell us where he was, of course, so Dad listened to the news for the rest of the war trying to figure out where George was. He guessed they were bombing over Italy, and that turned out to be right.

Although we didn't have alcohol as we were growing up, Dad had a bottle of rum in the top of the kitchen cabinet. If he got up with a sore throat at four or four thirty, he would take a swig out of that bottle. I guess it worked—he never had a cold.

There was a barrel in the cellar full of cider. It would stay sweet if it was vented, which meant running a hose from the cider out of the barrel into a pail of water, but some of Dad's friends he played checkers with on Saturday night wanted hard cider, so he would stop venting it. Eventually it turned hard, and the checkers games became more lively. He played checkers scientifically, hard cider or not, and usually won. He knew your next move and his next move. His friends were constantly trying to beat him. If he lost, he said he got careless.

He liked fishing, but didn't get many chances. My brothers used to take him fishing for the weekend at Moosehead Lake while my brother-in-law Jud came and milked the cows and did the chores. They would do that about three times during the summer unless the haying was behind.

Dad liked boxing and wrestling and so did my Mom (she recorded in her diary the outcomes of the fights), so, because we didn't have electricity, didn't have TV, we used to go to Perkins's and watch the fights with Carroll and Susie on Saturday night.

Afterward, there would always be refreshments, usually cupcakes or cookies, and coffee or tea.

CHAPTER THREE

Ida (Mclain) Ames

My Mom, Ida McLain, was born on June 28, 1893, in Worcester, Massachusetts, but grew up in Bath where her father, John, was a policeman. Her parents divorced when she was seven, and the four children in the family were parceled out to various relatives. The McLain homestead was in Waldoboro, and John's sister, who also lived in Bath, adopted Mom. Her mother continued to maintain a boarding house in Bath, and had three male boarders who worked at Bath Iron Works.

After Mom graduated from Morse High (then called Bath High), she took a job as a telephone operator at New England Telephone Company. She was talented musically and played the organ at her church in Bath, which is where she and Dad were introduced by a mutual friend. When they were married, she was 19, almost 20, didn't know how to cook, and had never lived on a farm.

> When the phone was picked up to make a call, the operator came on the line to ask what number you were calling, then made the connections manually on a big switchboard.

That would change, but not right away. First, she and my Dad would spend a couple of years in Skowhegan where Dad had a job as a mechanic at the Maine State Garage. In the meantime, my grandmother was living at the farm.

When Mom became pregnant with my sister Ruth, they moved back to the farm. My grandmother taught her how to cook, and she would become a fabulous cook. She learned about farming and canning, and running a farm household, from Dad and his mother.

Ruth was sixteen, had planned to get a job in town, and was upset with Mom when she became pregnant with me and told her she would need her at home to help out. Ruth said she would only forgive her if I was a girl. She became like a second mother to me, and I adored her.

Meantime, the family was growing. My brother Harold was born in 1916, a year after Ruth. My brother Gilbert was born in 1921, and my brother George was born in 1924. Dad was building his herd of cattle and cutting wood to sell. I was born in 1931.

That was a lot of mouths to feed, and the food had to be on hand and preserved. Using ice would work for the short term, but we didn't have any freezers. Canning was the only way of preserving meat and vegetables at that time. Mom picked the peas and beans we canned. Except for chicken, game was the only meat that was canned.

We used the old-fashioned glass jars with bails and jar rubbers for canning. Everything that's canned is cooked before it's put in jars, and then it's processed to seal the jars. That means putting the full jars into a covered canner and boiling for two to three hours. The bails on the jars were left in an up position until the jars were removed from the boiling water. Then the bails were locked down to complete the seal.

We couldn't afford to buy meat to can. We got protein from eggs, bacon, baked beans.

The original Colonial stairs to the cellar still exist and have been repurposed. Both the sides and the steps are solid pine slabs. The sides are notched and the steps fitted into the notches. The sides are held together with rounded wooden rods.

We had a cellar under the parlor that went to the front foundation. There was a room in the cellar with shelves where all the canned goods were kept. We went into each winter with at least 500 cans of food (fewer after there were only three of us). The canning increased as the family grew, and her biggest year was close to 1000 jars of vegetables, chickens, and deer meat.

Carrots and beets were kept whole in that cellar in bins.

We ate well, thanks to Mom's good cooking, three full meals every day. With all the hard work we did, we needed it. After early-morning chores, Dad had bacon, eggs, home fries, and biscuits for breakfast, plus a donut or two. Dinner, at twelve noon, was a full meal and supper was a full meal, so she was cooking a good portion of the day. She made fresh donuts every Saturday, and everyone lined up for donut holes that she made especially for us. She used a pot of shortening on the woodstove for frying the donuts.

He also liked applesauce with his biscuits. Mom canned applesauce so that we always had some available.

She baked beans every Saturday in the woodstove and made brown bread or biscuits to go with them. Sometimes we had ham with the beans. That was Sunday morning breakfast, also. When the uncles and aunts came to visit, she would insist they eat with us and proceed to get a meal together. Sometimes it was pancakes or waffles and ham or bacon. Think they had that in mind when they decided to visit on Saturday or Sunday, mostly Sunday evening.

On Sundays, summer or winter, it was also homemade ice cream.

As Dad's herd of cattle grew and the quantity of milk grew, she made butter and sold some of it.

There was a crabapple tree right on the other side of the driveway just toward the stable from where the flagpole is, usually full of crab-apples. She would make a simple syrup and preserve the apples in it with the stems on. Dad loved them with pork chops.

We had a grape arbor beside the stable loaded with Concord grapes each fall. I thought they were sour, but she made grape jelly with them. There was a cherry tree near where the flagpole is and they were also sour, but Mom used to use them. Not much was wasted.

On wash day, we carried water from the stable pump to the kitchen for washing. We had a tub in the kitchen, divided in two parts. She had a large bucket that she used to heat part of the water, used on one side of the tub, and the cold water for rinsing was put in the other side. All of the clothes had to be washed by hand, sheets included. They had to be hung on the clothesline to dry, summer and winter. I remember the sheets being frozen solid. There were a few clothes racks to use to finish drying them.

She sewed a lot of our clothes and crocheted newborn baby clothes and women's bed jackets for some company that sold them in Boston.

Bed jackets were a fashionable item for women in the 1940s. They were used for extra warmth, both in and out of bed.

She knitted mittens and hats for all of us. She liked to listen to soaps during the day while she sat and crocheted her baby clothes, and she always had on a radio with a huge battery. We had to have two batteries so that we had a spare for when one lost its juice. Dad had to take the battery to Bath to be charged, but sometimes our neighbor, Horace Allen, would take one of the batteries to be recharged for us.

She did so many things at our farm that I still don't know how she found the time for them all.

And there was still more.

Mom enjoyed being with other people, and there was a lot more sociability then than I think there is now. The farm never seemed isolated, and people always visited. Everyone knew my parents, and we knew most people in town. They both always went to Town Meeting.

In the 1938 Town Meeting, when I was seven, she was elected to the School Committee for the first time ("on the fourth ballot," according to her diary). Reelected to three more three-year terms, she chaired the committee during most of that time. There was a "union" of School Committees during that period among Woolwich, Waldoboro, and Warren called Union 48, and in 1946, she was elected secretary of the union. Dad had to take her to the meetings, as she never drove. I remember going to meetings and sleeping on the couch while they had the meeting. There were few meetings at the farm because we didn't have power and good lighting.

She tried to learn, but when she ran the car into the house, Dad said, "No more." He tried to joke with her about it, but she wouldn't think he was joking and would get upset. He would just chuckle and go back to work.

Mom didn't talk about her School Committee work very much at all, even with Dad, but it meant a lot to her to be asked to serve. She was a smart woman, and this was her opportunity to do something important besides her work at the farm.

CHAPTER FOUR

The Farm and Farm Buildings

Courtesey Woolwich Historical Society

Our farmhouse sat on high ground, and so when the river flooded in 1937, we were on an island and had to row to get to dry land.

The main house had four large rooms, two on each floor, each one having original pine floor boards ten to seventeen inches wide running front to back. The room to the left of the front door was used as a spare bedroom. On the right was the parlor. On the floor above on the left was the summer bedroom for one or more of us kids and on the right was my parents' summer bedroom. There was a narrow set of stairs from the front door to the second floor and on up to the attic, where there was a trapdoor.

A long ell went back from the main house toward the stable. A side door into the ell opened into our living room, from which one door opened into the dining room and another door opened into the kitchen and a big pantry

> There was never very much up in the attic. My father's mother was gone before I was born, but I used to have a dream that when I opened the door to the attic, she would be there to greet me.

Ames Homestead – Winter, 1940.

where Mom did all of the food prep. She cooked on a woodstove, so the kitchen was always warm, but the floor of the pantry—where the icebox and the flour barrel were—was cold because there was no cellar under it. The flour barrel held at least 50 pounds of flour.

The icebox was made of oak with a big compartment on the top right side lined with metal, I think aluminum, to hold the ice. It held half a cake of ice that lasted three or four days before another chunk had to be hauled from the ice stack on a sled or a wheelbarrow and put in. The rest of the box was white porcelain and easy to keep clean. There was a pan on the bottom that caught the melt from the ice cake.

> We didn't have as much need for an icebox then as we do now for a refrigerator. Mom was very good at portion control, and there wasn't much uneaten food left over after a meal. Of course, we all had good appetites, too.

A door at the end of the kitchen opened into the shed, where the wood was stored (and where deer, when we shot them, were hung until Dad butchered them). Our privy was off an alleyway from the shed that led to stairs into the stable.

Dad had a workbench inside the outside wall of the stable, and large cabinets for items like the harnesses, shoes, etc., for the horses. From there, a sliding door went in to the horses. There were shutters in front of the horses that opened down to a trough so they could be fed grain and water. Their hay was

> The privy was always used as long as my parents lived there, as they couldn't afford to have a bathroom installed. My father hauled the waste away, but I'm not sure where. It was not used on the fields.

kept in the loft overhead. A hand pump in the corner of the stable brought water for us and the horses from a dug well about a couple of dozen yards out from the corner of the stable. We pumped water into the trough in front of the horses and into pails we carried into the house, where the water could be used for everything we needed.

The one pig we raised each year was kept in a pen under the part of the stable where the horses lived, until late fall when it would be big enough for Dad to slaughter into quarters.

All of the main house and the ell were used in the good weather. In winter, when it got cold, only four rooms were used. (Sometimes it got cold enough the top of the water in the pail would freeze over at night.) My parents took their bed apart, carried the parts downstairs, and reassembled it in the parlor to sleep in the winter. Their upstairs bedroom opened into a small winter bedroom—a loft over the ell—for us kids and stairs down into our living room on the first floor.

We heated with two stoves, the cookstove, which burned wood, and the parlor heater in the living room, which burned coal. The cookstove was a Home Comfort cast-iron stove, bought direct from the company through one of its traveling salesmen. You couldn't buy one at retail.

The firebox in a Home Comfort cookstove (where the stove wood goes) is on the left side of the stove, and the oven is behind the big door. In the middle of the oven door was a thermometer that told you how hot it was in the oven. There were either six or eight covers on the stove top, depending on the size of the stove. My Mom's stove had eight.

I've always thought that 400-degree heat in a Home Comfort oven was different (and better) than in an electric oven. It went further and made you more comfortable.

The heat in the oven and on the stove top was regulated by the draft (the amount of air

A "cover" is a round iron disc that fits into the top of the cookstove and has a notch in it into which the end of the "lifter" fits. The lifter is a metal handle whose other end, when fitted into the notch, allows you to lift the iron disc and put it to one side temporarily, leaving an open hole down into the firebox. In order to feed stove wood into the firebox, both covers on the left side had to be lifted, as well as the iron piece between them, which was also notched. The covers other than those on the left side would be lifted in order to clean the inside of that part of the stove.

you let into the firebox), which would determine the temperature the wood was generating. The draft was regulated in several ways, by opening the left side door on the stove that opened down (you could also feed small sticks of wood in through this door, not big ones). There were other controls, on the middle drawer in the left side, and on the stack to the rear of the stove. The ashes fell through a grate and were taken out through the two doors at the bottom of the stove.

There was a water tank hooked onto, and next to, the left side of the stove. That was the source of our hot water, whether to wash or to do dishes or to bathe. It held probably ten gallons, and got up to around 180 degrees—warm enough, but not too warm. There was a rack off the right side on which you could put dishes or pots or pans, with a round bar at the outside for dish cloths that needed to be dried.

The two boxes on either side at the top of the stove were warming ovens that kept food warm while other food was cooking. Mom had to keep track of whatever was happening in the kitchen. The cookstove had to be kept going all year round, even in the middle of summer heat. And Mom had to be in the middle of it, all year round.

The fuel for the parlor heater, which my Mom also tended, was coal. She added coal to the heater twice a day. It was kept burning from fall to spring. The parlor heater was a round black stove about five feet tall. The stovepipe went into the chimney opposite from the kitchen stove. The kitchen stove used wood and would burn out almost every night. There was a register in the ceiling over the coal stove so some heat would go up to the little winter bedroom where we kids slept.

There was a separate, smaller house attached to the main house. We called it "the other part," and I was told it was built as a grandparents' house. The "other part" was used for a lot of things. It had a kitchen, living room, bedroom, and pantry downstairs and four small bedrooms upstairs. There was a fireplace that provided heat. Mom liked her Home Comfort woodstove so much that Dad bought a smaller one for

There were four men who used to stay there for two weeks in the fall for the sole purpose of hunting. Dad was a Maine Guide and took them duck and deer hunting.

the kitchen in the "other part." There was also a Dutch oven for the kitchen. It was used by us kids when we first got married. I lived there for about two years. I imagine it could have been used as quarters for men in the ice trade in the 1800s, but I never heard any report of that.

About halfway between the "other part" and the barn was the milk house where we took the milk pails after the cows had been milked to strain any impurities out of the milk, pour the milk into the milk cans we took to the dairy, and keep the milk cool until then. The milk house was a shingled building about ten feet by eight feet, with a pitched, shingled roof, a couple of small windows, a door on one shorter end, and a concrete floor. Dad had poured the concrete, built the building, and shingled it, sides and roof.

The barn was about sixty feet long and about twenty-five feet to the peak of the roof. It had big doors on the river end so you could tow the hay rack in to be unloaded, or bring in the grain and fodder corn for the cattle that was stored in a room just inside the big doors. The farm machinery would be kept in there for the winter, and also the ice harvesting gear. Otherwise the big doors stayed closed.

About halfway along the side of the barn toward the house was a ramp leading to the smaller cattle doors and the linter that took up about two-thirds of the floor space on that side of the barn. The linter was enclosed and roofed, the roof serving as a floor for a part of the hay mow. Each cow had its own stall and a trough in front of it for water, hay, and fodder. Behind each cow was a board in the floor you could lift to shovel the manure down to the barn basement (which was no wider than the cows' area).

The linter in the barn is the part where the cows had their stalls. I know "linter" is not much used now, but we always used it to describe that area.

There was a henhouse at the end of the barn and beyond that, the pump house over the dug well where we got the water for the cattle. We had about twelve hens—no rooster. Dad borrowed a rooster when he wanted to raise some chickens. When the hens got to be five or six years old, we replaced them with young ones and ate the hens. There was a ramp that led from the henhouse to the ground, where there was a fenced-in yard for them.

When Jacob Eames bought the farm in 1779, there was a rangeway on it some distance north of the barn that cut east across our field toward the watercourse we called "the swamp," and then went gradually straight uphill some considerable distance until it met what was then the main road. The rangeway was our driveway before the Feds built that part of the River Road that cut across our farm, which was when the three farms got together on a single driveway—George Ames Road—to the new road.

Rangeways were included in the lots that the Kennebec Proprietors and other land speculators along the Kennebec River sold to assure access to the new owners and their successors.

Our field and the adjoining Hathorn and Thwing fields had once been river bottom, and the soil was rich. You could grow anything there. It was a big field. We grew hay for the animals there and raised cash crops to sell and for our own food.

The swamp wasn't really a swamp but a shallow watercourse that started out from the river some distance north of our farm and cut through Hathorns' and our farm and the Thwing and Reed farms on its way back to the river. Like the river, it was tidal, and probably was once part of the river bottom that made our soil so rich. Ducks and geese and herons used it, along with snapping turtles and peepers (little tree frogs) in the spring.

I was too young to see it, but my sister and my brothers—and my Dad and Mom—played baseball in one part of the field. Every town around had a town team, and the towns would play each other on different fields in the summer. Our field was the Woolwich field for a few years.

Our pastures for the cows were on the other side of the swamp, so we'd have to get them over there after morning milking. We had a twenty-foot lane with fencing on both sides from the barn to the swamp, where it joined the rangeway. There was a wooden bridge on the rangeway across the swamp that Dad kept up. He'd brought gravel in to put on both sides so the bridge didn't have to span a long distance, but sometimes in the spring we'd find the ice had sprung the boards.

The "home pasture" went from the swamp up to the River Road after it was built, and from there north to Perkins just before the Dresden line. Before the River Road, it went all the way up to the old main road we afterwards called the "back road." We didn't take the cattle

My bedroom had windows on both sides that I'd leave open in the spring. I could hear ducks and geese flying up the river on the one side and peepers on the other.

across the River Road because there was plenty of room for them in the home pasture, and they could drink from the swamp. The home pasture had a lot of trees for shade and was open enough so the cows were comfortable.

The land between the River Road and the back road was the middle pasture, and our land on the other side of the back road was the "back pasture." It was a large piece of land and went almost all the way to Middle Road and was bordered by what used to be Murphy. Our heifers—there would be six or eight of them—stayed in the back pasture in all the warm weather. We went up and called them to come and get grain, and they always did.

The other side of the farm from our house faced the Kennebec River. The riverbank was a hundred yards away from the front door, across a field just beyond a little brick building the Coast Guard owned, where they had kept kerosene and spare parts for the warning light they put another hundred yards out in the river on what they called "Ames Ledge" and we called the "island." With boots on, you could walk out to the island at low tide.

My family had tended the light since it was put out there in the late 1800s after (I was told) a barge had fetched up on the ledge and lost its load. There used to be a fair amount of barge traffic coming downriver,

Looking out past the Coast Guard building to Ames Ledge.

including from the Hallowell granite quarries. Our barn had a granite foundation, which was unusual. Someone said it looked like Hallowell granite, but I wouldn't know about that.

My grandmother had tended the light and, after her, Dad did, until the Coast Guard decided to replace the light with a keg on a pole. (I was very young when that happened.) The Coast Guard abandoned the building then, since it no longer needed to store supplies there for the light, and, twenty years having passed, its ownership reverted back to the landowner.

However, the Coast Guard still owned a right-of-way across our land to get to the building, and the right-of-way didn't revert. According to government regulations, it had to be put up for bid and advertised nationwide. Dad couldn't take a chance on someone else getting it, so he had to buy it. He had no idea how much to bid so it cost him a lot more than it should have, more than he could afford. Seems like it shouldn't have cost him anything after all those years of our family tending the light.

—————◦◦◦◦—————

CHAPTER FIVE

Doing the Chores and Tending the Cows

Mornings began early. We were up at 4:30 a.m. and out to the barn to get chores done before breakfast. We shoveled out behind the cows and put fresh sawdust down under them. There was a board behind each cow that we lifted to shovel the manure into the cellar, where it stayed until spring. We got hay down on the barn floor for later, put grain in the boxes, and got the milking machine ready to use.

Before we had power, a gasoline engine ran the milking machine. The milking machine was a pail with a hose and four teat cups attached. There was an air hose that ran above the cows' heads that we attached the teat cup hose to, and the vacuum would

Orrin Perkins's brother Gus had a manure spreader he would bring down every spring and help Dad shovel the manure out of the cellar and spread it on the fields.

create a pulsing action to resemble a hand milking them. It took about ten to fifteen minutes per cow to milk them. Dad had hand-milked the cows before he got the milking machine, and it had been hard for the cows to adjust to the machine. I remember one that didn't adjust—she would kick off the hose, and the noise would frighten her—so Dad had to continue to milk her by hand. Another one or two also had to be hand-milked because they wouldn't release their milk with the machine on.

The cows produced better with music when we milked them, so we always had a radio playing.

We carried their milk from the barn to the milk house in pails to pour into the big cans we drove to the dairy. Opposite the door to the milk house and across the cement floor was a big straight-sided cooler tank. The tank was about six feet by four feet and four feet high, held water and ice from the ice stack, and had room for about eight eight-gallon milk cans.

To get rid of any impurities, we first strained the milk from the pails into the cans through cheesecloth in a big funnel. Once full, the cans then had to be lifted and put into the ice water inside the cooler tank. In summer, when the ice melted, it would have to be replenished, and the excess water was drained out of the tank through a faucet attached to a hose. Didn't have to worry about that much in winter, but the water temp in the tank had to be maintained at below 35 degrees year round so we always checked it, especially after the afternoon milking, since that milk stayed in the cooler until next morning after breakfast.

A lot of ice got hauled from the ice stack to the milk house.

Brucellosis was a major concern because it could be transmitted to humans and other animals. We were told that halitosis (bad breath) in cows could be an early sign of brucellosis, which raised the level of our worry because cows aren't known for their sweet breath. Halitosis in cows can be a sign of other conditions as well.

There was a big problem in the state with brucellosis in cows at about that time, and the state notified all dairy farmers their cows would have to be tested for it. One of our cows tested positive, and the state's Animal Husbandry department recommended that we treat it by feeding the cow a mixture of molasses and honey, mixed with some water to make it more fluid, twice a day for three days, and then have the cow tested again. Dad decided we should mix in about three tablespoons of rum, and that's what we did. At the end of the three days, the cow was tested again, and it was cured. Dad figured it was the rum.

In the meantime, that cow was segregated, and we couldn't deliver its milk to the dairy. Dad dug a hole, which is where its milk went. We never had an issue with any other cow.

At some point, the dairy shifted over from eight-gallon to twelve-gallon cans, which were more than half as tall as Dad was and couldn't be lifted into the cooler tank by hand. The twelve-gallon tanks had rugged handles, one on each side, so he rigged up a rope hung from a pulley attached to a beam halfway across the milk house ceiling. The rope went down to a set of ice tongs he closed around the handles. Using the pulley, he could lift the cans up into the cooler tank and lift them out again.

Filling the cans to take to the dairy was a continuous process. Once the pails had been emptied into the cans and the cans put in the cooler tank, we took the empty pails back to the barn to be filled up again, until the cows were done. When the cows were done, we could leave the cans in the cooler tank, take the pails inside to be washed, and go have breakfast.

The chores took about two hours, and Mom would have breakfast ready for us when we were done. Bacon, eggs, home fries, biscuits, and usually homemade donuts. We had to eat three full meals a day with the kind of work we did, and this was just the first one.

After breakfast, we went out to give the cows water. There was a pump house about fifty feet from the east corner of the barn sitting over a twenty-foot-deep dug well. We had a gas-powered pump to pump the water from the well to the barn, but there was a time when the water had to be pumped by hand, and the hand pump was still in the pump house in case it was needed. The water went into troughs in the barn in front of the cattle. We had to keep the troughs covered so the cattle wouldn't slop the water all over.

After all that, when I was still in school, I'd head off while someone else took the milk to the dairy. Later, when I was done with school and back living in the house, most of the time that was me.

We drove the milk to the dairy in the trunk of my grandmother's Oldsmobile. It was a big trunk, and when we were dealing with the smaller milk cans, we could close the lid with them standing up inside. Not with the big cans. Then, we'd stand the big cans, usually three of them (more in the summer), up in the trunk, put the lid down over them, and use a rope to tie the lid of the trunk to the rear bumper.

The empty pails and the empty cans brought back from the dairy were washed every day. Mom did that. Once washed, they were put on a long shelf in the milk house along the wall to the right of the

The cows would produce more milk in the summer because of the great feed they got grazing in the pasture. There would also be more milk, depending on when Dad bred the heifers.

door until the next milking, which would be around 5 p.m. Except that the afternoon milk wouldn't be taken to the dairy until after breakfast next morning, we followed the same routine with each milking.

Seven days a week.

After the milk had been delivered, the rest of my day was spent doing whatever was on the schedule for that time of year: in the spring, planting, cultivating, weeding; in the summer, haying and harvesting; in the winter, shoveling, cutting the wood to fill the shed for the stoves. Didn't have much "me" time.

After they'd been milked and fed, the cattle would be let out of the barn to go to pasture. There was a fenced lane that led across the field and the bridge over the bog to the pastures, and that's where they spent their days. The cattle didn't need to rely on food from the pasture but mostly browsed around and slept in the shade. The pastures were also fenced in all the way around. The new River Road had divided our pastures, so the cow pasture stopped at the main road. That pasture once had a lot of space free of trees. Looks different now, because the young trees weren't cut down as they grew.

There was no need to go get the cows from the pasture. They knew when the time was to come back to the barn, and a clock could be set to the time of their return. In the meantime, we had pumped water into a large trough in the barnyard for the cattle to drink from when they came back. There was always a lead cow (no idea who among them chose her), and when they'd had their water and the door for the cows on the side of the barn was opened, they would follow her in and go right into their own stalls. Cows are creatures of habit.

We had twenty-five or -six cows, calves, and heifers in the barn, plus the bull. We milked fourteen or fifteen cows and they were milked twice a day. Each cow averaged fifteen to twenty quarts per milking, depending where they were in their cycle. Their milk production diminished as they got nearer to their next calf birth. Their span for production was seven to eight years. Most of the cows were Guernseys. Their milk is the second richest in butterfat content. Jerseys have the highest content of butterfat, and we had two of them. Holsteins have the lowest content of butterfat but give larger amounts of milk per cow, so we had a couple of them to balance out the butterfat. The higher butterfat content brought us more money per pound.

We always had six to eight two-year-old heifers and about the same number of calves to raise. A heifer becomes a cow at about two years old, when she's bred to the bull and starts to give milk. The heifers were waiting to replace an aging cow, and the calves were being raised to replace the heifers as they replaced the cows, so there was a sort of recycling going on. We kept all of the female calves, but the bull calves were sold for ten or fifteen dollars apiece. The bottom line was maintenance of milk production.

The heifers were pastured out in the summer. There were a couple of places that had fenced-in pastures and took young cattle for the summer for a small fee. We used the back pasture for them until it got too grown up with trees and too hard to fence. It was quite the project to maintain the fence around that pasture.

The calves stayed in the barn and lived in a large pen on one end. The heifers lived in the other end in the pen where the milking machine was kept. There was a door in that pen that opened into the henhouse next to that end of the barn, where we kept a dozen or so hens. About once or twice a year we would let a hen hatch a nest of eggs to be used for eating and replacing the older hens. My mother had to can the replaced hens to preserve them.

As a cow was approaching the birth of a calf, Dad tried to keep it in the barn, but once in a while a calf would be born in the pasture. It was usually hidden pretty well, so it was very difficult to find. The cow would bring it to the barn after a few days, but the cow would need to be milked because the calf couldn't drink it all, and the cow needed to be relieved of the pressure of so much milk. Even though we milked her, we couldn't use her milk until three or four days after the birth.

The bull was tied up at the end of the line of cows. He had a permanent ring in his nose for leading. Carroll Perkins would walk his cow down to be serviced and so would Orrin Perkins. The bull was kept busy.

———➤●◄———

CHAPTER SIX

Bob and Frank: The Horses

Horses were necessary to the operation of the farm until Dad built the tractor. We had a team of draft horses, Bob and Frank, just a size smaller than Belgians. I have no idea where their names came from, but they were Bob and Frank. They were perfectly matched—roan with white stripes down their faces.

They were gentle giants, and well trained. Dad would unhook them from the machinery and tell them to go to the stable, sometimes put me on their back, and they would go into the stable on their own and wait for him to come unharness them. They allowed him to change their shoes twice a year with no objection. (Each one would place a hoof in his lap and wait patiently while he pulled out the nails holding the old shoe, then nailed the new one back on.) At the same time, he had to trim their hoof nails, using large cutting pliers. I used to watch. Their winter shoes had studs that would keep them from slipping on the ice. Their summer shoes were flatter, and that was also to protect the pavement.

Before we had a tractor, it took a lot longer to till the ground with the horses, so we couldn't grow as much. We only had time to grow what we needed.

The team was used to plow the ground and harrow it. One horse was used to make furrows for planting and cultivating the vegetable garden. The fences had to be checked and restored for the summer, and Frank would pull a cart with the fence stakes and wire. After the fencing was done, the cattle could be turned into the pasture.

The team was used for mowing the hay, and one horse was used for raking hay into windrows or piles. One horse was used to haul the hay rack so we could load it, then pull it to the barn to stow away the hay. There was a hay fork that took the hay from the load to the scaffold in the top of the barn. There was a rope connected to the hay fork, and the horse would pull the rope out to lift the hay to the top of the barn. There was a lot of work for the horses to do.

The major projects for winter where we needed the horses were harvesting ice and filling up our icehouse and cutting firewood for the next year. When he was cutting wood, Dad would take the horse and dog up to the middle pasture for the day.

We had blankets for the horses when it was very cold. The space where they lived was small and closed in, so it didn't get terribly cold. Their bodies were quite warm.

We didn't have a snowplow for the truck. When I was little, Dad had a plow that the horses pulled around the house to the barn to keep the roadway clear, but after we lost one of the team, that didn't work anymore.

There weren't any veterinarians around, and there were no medications that would help. Farmers knew their animals, and Dad knew there was nothing that could be done. It was some years later when a vet came to Brunswick.

Bob was about fourteen years old when he got sick. He got colic, and it was so bad he couldn't recover from it, so Dad had to put him down. Dad loved that horse and was heartbroken. Only saw Dad cry twice and that was one of them.

The other horse, Frank, refused to haul Bob down the hill toward the swamp, where we buried him, and he would call to Bob, whinny, for a long time after that, at least a couple of weeks. That was the first lesson of animal grieving I experienced.

Horace Allen brought his tractor down to haul Bob to the place near the swamp that Dad had dug for him. That's where he is.

Frank was the one that worked best alone, however. He pulled the mowing machine to cut the hay, then the rake to rake the hay, the plow to plow the gardens, the harrow to harrow the soil, the hay rack to haul the hay to the barn, and the cultivator to keep the soil clear of weeds. He was also used to pull the hay to the top of the barn when it was being unloaded.

Frank never offered to eat the hay or any of the veggies when cultivating. Can't remember how old he was when Dad sold him, but he was pretty old by then. Dad bought another horse to use for pulling the hay up and for cultivating—and that horse would eat anything and would not stay between the rows when cultivating.

CHAPTER SEVEN

Building the Tractor

Up until Bob died in 1941, the horses had done all the hauling that needed to be done, from plowing in the spring to hauling ice to the ice stack in winter. Although Dad would replace Bob, Frank was old, and Dad decided we needed to have a tractor. Since he couldn't afford to buy one—even used—he set about building one.

Before I was born, we had a one-horse buggy. Mom used to drive it to Bath when she needed something, or if she wanted to visit her mother. I used to see it in the barn.

We had two vehicles at the time. One was a ten- or fifteen-year-old dump truck with a Model A engine Dad had bought used that he needed for his job as Road Commissioner. (Great engine. He kept it going, and we had it forever.) The other was a 1928 or 1929 Model A four-door sedan he'd bought earlier, also secondhand, that we used for transportation. (I learned to drive in the Model A when I could barely reach the pedals.) We needed both, but Dad had a mechanic friend who offered him an old Ford coupe for forty-five dollars, and he took it.

Dad spent a good part of that winter building the tractor, using an oxyacetylene torch he had for cutting and welding. I've no idea where and how he'd learned to use it, but he always seemed to be able to do what needed to be done, and this was no exception. He had two fuel tanks for the torch, one of them always full.

One tank held liquid oxygen, the other the acetylene. The combination gives you the hot flame needed for cutting steel and for welding.

He used goggles when he was working with it, not one of those full-face shields they have now. I'd watch, sometimes, but he'd never let me get close. The light was too bright, he said.

First, he cut the outside body off, keeping the chassis and the hood, then he took out the seats and added a trailer hitch on the rear. For the driver's seat, still on the left side behind the wheel, he decided to use the seat from the dump rake. The dump rake seat was mounted on a flexible post. Mounted on the tractor, we could lean a little if we were sideways on a rise to compensate and help keep the tractor upright.

The dump rake, when used behind horses, is ridden. There are curved tines that reach down to the ground to pick up hay after it's been cut and dried. The tines hold the hay while you take the rake to where you want to dump the hay. From there it will be forked onto the hay rack and taken to the barn. To dump the hay, there was a lever beside the seat that was pulled to lift up the tines.

The seat on a dump rake was metal, but it was contoured to fit your bottom, so it was comfortable. And since its post was flexible, it was easy on the body.

Since the horses were going to be replaced with a tractor, nobody was going to ride the dump rake anymore, and it wouldn't need its seat. It also wasn't going to need the tongue that connected to the horses, so Dad cut that off and made a piece that would connect the rake to the trailer hitch on the back of the tractor. He then rigged up a rope from the dump lever forward to the driver's seat on the tractor so the driver could lift up the tines by pulling on the rope and dump the hay where he wanted it.

A sulky dump rake that could be operated with one horse.
© Can Stock Photo/rjfiskness

With the driver behind the wheel on one side of the tractor, he still needed to balance off the driver, so he put in a thirty-inch-square cement block on what used to be the passenger side of the car.

I drove everything we had that was drivable from about the age of 11 or 12, including the tractor. The biggest thing about the tractor was I had to learn to maneuver on the hill over by the Hathorn cellar hole. Couldn't drive it sideways on the hill because it was top-heavy and might tip. Had to drive it straight up and straight down. Can't drive anything sideways on a hill safely.

I drove the tractor for whatever needed to be done, including in all parts of the haying operation, starting with cutting. We had a bar mower which attached under the tractor, with the bar extended out on the passenger side. The bar had two rows of teeth sharpened on the sides that went back and forth and worked sort of like scissors to cut the hay. They weren't pointed in the front, just sharpened on the sides. When we were mowing hay, the teeth would dull, and Dad had to sharpen both sides of each one by hand at least once a week. Dad did most of the mowing.

The tractor he built that winter was with us forever. You couldn't kill those old Ford motors, no matter if you tried. Later on, when I was older and living at the farm, and we didn't have my brothers' regular help, Dad bought a used Allis-Chalmers tractor. We were able to use both tractors at the same time and cover more ground.

—————◦►◦◄◦—————

CHAPTER EIGHT

Spring, Summer, and Cash Crops

The more frost there is in the ground, the longer it takes in the spring for the ground to be tillable, and the amount of frost was dependent on how early the snow had come. When the snow was gone and the frost was all out of the ground, we would start plowing ground to plant the crops—and we'd have mud season.

Mud season would last about two or three weeks toward the end of March, depending on the weather. Coming down the hill from the main road was so muddy we had to leave the car up at Horace Allen's and use the dump truck to take the milk out to the car. There were other places along the road coming in to the farm you wouldn't want to drive through. We had to stock up on grain for the cows so we would have enough to get us through. If we had a lot of sun, the mud would dry up sooner.

We'd keep an ear out then for the peepers in the swamp. Dad and I used to compete about who would hear the first peeper. Some years we could hear them for the first time on April Fool's Day. One of us would go to the door toward the barn and listen and say we heard them, then call to the other. If they weren't peeping when the other came, it would be "April Fool!" And a big laugh.

Our "peepers" were tiny frogs that climbed trees around the swamp in spring and made shrill "peeping" sounds. There were lots of them, and some years they got so loud it was the only thing you could hear.

The peepers were one of God's creatures, and apart from having fun with us about them, Dad made sure we knew that God created all living things and we needed to help God by taking care of his creatures.

We weren't able to go to church often, for a lot of reasons, but Mom had been a Sunday school teacher, and she taught us about Jesus and his teachings. Mom made sure that we grew up living with Jesus, and that he lived with us.

Birds were God's special creatures, and they lived with us, too. They were special in spring when they were nesting, but they were always with us. During winter, we had chickadees, of course, titmice and blue jays, and usually a cardinal pair bright red against the snow, and sparrows wintering over. Then, in spring, the robins would come, along with swallows and doves, goldfinches, red-winged blackbirds, starlings, bob-o-links, brown-headed cowbirds, catbirds, woodpeckers and flickers, maybe, and sometimes a bluebird or rose-breasted grosbeak, or an oriole. Ospreys circled and fished in the river, and red-tailed hawks hunted in our fields.

Dad built three birdhouses in the yard perched on tall poles he'd cut from cedar stalks. Cats and raccoons would want to climb the poles to get at the birds, so he ringed the poles with tin collars about three feet wide to keep them off. We'd have swallows in the birdhouses, and maybe a phoebe, but phoebes preferred to make their nests under roof overhangs if they could find a place to anchor them.

We had "barn" swallows coming through the cracks and nesting in the barn, but that wasn't the only place. Somehow they got into the shed between the kitchen and the stable to build nests. So we left the north door to the shed open for them to come in. Sometimes they had two nestings in a season.

What was fun for us was that a pair of house finches would usually make their nest in the purple lilac bush outside the parlor. We could watch them through the window hatching and feeding the chicks, and we were careful not to make noise. They were contented to be there. It was especially interesting to watch when it was time for the mother to help the chicks leave the nest. She would stop feeding them—so they had to find their own food—and fly up into the big crabapple tree to perch and watch them while they did.

❖

One of the first chores every spring, as soon as the frost was out of the ground, was to check the fencing and repair it if necessary. There was no point in doing it earlier because sometimes the frost would heave the wooden stakes clear out of the ground, and you had to be able to drive the old stake—or new ones—back into the ground. Dad made the fence stakes from small trees, preferably cedars. Cedar trees are more durable and don't rot like other trees do.

We used "cattle fencing," which consisted of two wires between the stakes. One person could do the fencing, but it was a lot easier and faster when there were two. The fences went from the barnyard down both sides of the lane the cows used to cross the field to the bridge over the swamp and into the home pasture. At the end of the bridge, one fence went in one direction and the other in the opposite direction. They circled the home pasture up to the River Road, where they met again in the middle. Before the River Road was built, the fence went all around the middle pasture as well. After the road was built, we stopped fencing the middle pasture and only fenced the home pasture on the farm side of the road.

The back pasture was also fenced so the heifers could be there in the summer. At some point, we stopped fencing the back pasture and the heifers were farmed out to other places for the summer.

Next was planting. April 8 was a special date for us for planting decisions. Mom and Dad were married on his 21st birthday on April 8. Some years it would be spring on April 8, and some years there would still be snow. On their 40th anniversary, the snow was all gone and some green grass was showing. On their 50th anniversary, there were still two feet of snow.

Sometimes it would be May before the ground was ready to be prepared for plowing, harrowing, and planting. As it got to be warm—last of April, early May—we would let the calves out in the barnyard to run and play. It was fun to watch them. We looked forward to letting the cows out for the first time.

Money was needed to buy grain for the cattle, food for the chickens, and seeds for planting (we saved some seeds and used our own potatoes to plant). The only money we had was from the sale of the milk to the dairy and from cash crops we planted to sell.

We raised cash crops toward the Hathorn place, acres of beans and cabbage and squash and cauliflower. Dry beans were a safe commodity because they were not perishable. We also raised some potatoes. We had a machine that dug the potatoes in the fall and placed them on top of the ground. It was usually Susie, Sylvia, Dad, and I who picked them up and put them in 50-pound bags.

There was a store on Westport that used to buy some of our produce. Morse's in Waldoboro used to buy cabbage for sauerkraut to sell, and a few stores in Bath bought some crops. Dad delivered things in his dump truck.

There was something planted everywhere there wasn't hay, even pumpkins we sold in November. We couldn't plant the pumpkins near the Hathorn place because there were woods nearby, and the deer would come out and nibble on the pumpkins and make them unsaleable.

When the ground was ready for tilling, the manure in the barn cellar had to be cleaned out and spread on the ground. Gus Perkins, Carroll's father, would bring his manure spreader down to use for spreading the manure and help in loading it. The spreader was a large box on wheels and there was a thrower on the rear that was connected to the wheels, and when a lever was pulled down, the wheels put the thrower in motion to spread the manure. The manure had to be loaded out of the barn cellar into the spreader by hand with shovels. It was a lot of work.

Some of the manure was spread on the fields to make the hay crop richer, and some was spread on the tilled ground before it was harrowed and prepared for planting. After Dad built the tractor, spreading the manure went a lot faster than waiting for the horses to pull the spreader. After the manure was all taken care of, the harrowing was next, and then the planting.

Harrowing breaks up the clods that are left behind after plowing and smooths out the soil before furrowing it and planting. We had two

Spring-tooth harrow. By Daniel Christensen, Wikimedia Commons

kinds of harrows that the horses—and later, the tractor—towed. One had vertical spikes evenly spaced on a horizontal bar and was usually used on soil that had been planted the prior year and didn't need replowing. The other was a spring-tooth harrow that had horizontal bars with rows of vertical springs ending in teeth that dug deeper in the soil. It was usually used on new soil that had been plowed and broken up the prior fall.

We grew three kinds of corn: sweet corn for us and for sale, fodder corn for the cattle, and popcorn for us. We had to plant them far away from each other so they wouldn't cross-pollinate and spoil the sweet corn, which was planted between the house and the river, near the Coast Guard building. We dried some of the corn for seed. We had a machine that had to be cranked by hand to take the corn off the ear.

We rotated crops every year so the soil wouldn't get depleted. The beans were particularly bad. We had to pull the bean plants every fall, plow them under elsewhere, and plant the beans in a different location. Hay was planted everywhere we weren't growing crops.

We planted about five acres of fodder corn for the cows to eat during the summer. The whole stalk was fed to them. It usually had small ears of corn on it. They really liked eating that after they came in from the pasture.

There was a man in town who always tried to beat us for fresh peas. He would plant his peas while there was still frost in the ground, but we still had ripe peas before he did. Our land by the river was the best.

The family garden was usually planted on Memorial Day weekend between the barn and the river. Peas, carrots, pole beans, beets, bush beans, cabbage, cauliflower, lettuce, tomatoes, cucumbers, and potatoes for ourselves. The potatoes were "hilled" to keep them from getting burned by the sun. The cauliflower didn't keep long and would turn yellow, so it would have to be canned. We grew what we needed for ourselves.

We had bins in the cellar for our potatoes, carrots, and beets. The cellar was nice and dry, so they kept well. Along about February or March, the potatoes had to be "sprouted." There is an underground cellar behind the Thwing house that Mabel used to let us use to store the potatoes, and the cabbage and cauliflower for sale. They kept very well there, but if there was a lot of snow, we couldn't always get the potatoes out until spring.

Dad loved popcorn. His favorite evening snack was popcorn and milk. We popped the corn on the stove in a long-handled wire basket popper. It had to be tended so you'd be there when it popped.

CHAPTER NINE

Gauging the Weather

Fishermen and farmers have to be weather predictors because a lot of what they do depends on the weather. Dad would change his priorities depending on what he thought the weather was going to do. If he thought it was going to rain and there was dried hay out on the ground, getting that hay into the barn was his priority.

They didn't rely so much on weathermen for the pending weather because those forecasts weren't localized, and weather is. They relied on the kind of weather signs that had been passed down to them to make their own predictions, and those predictions were usually more accurate. They knew, for instance, that a storm from the nor'east lasts for three days, no matter what the weatherman says.

Wind direction had a lot to do with predicting weather. If it came from the west or northwest, the weather would be cool and clear. Warm and sunny weather came from the southwest. If it came from the east or northeast, you had to be on the lookout because the weather coming in could be anything.

Dad believed the weather on the first day of the season was a sign of what the average prevailing weather will be for that season. I remember one year the weather on the first day of winter was snow, sleet, and rain. That was the typical weather of that season.

Farmers didn't let the weather bother them any, but they took precautions, especially with summer thunderstorms. Dad was not afraid of thunderstorms, but he knew thunderstorms followed the river and would be most severe on the side of the river where we were.

Mom was fearful of thunderstorms. Dad would try to be with her when there was a severe one around.

He taught us how to be safe. Usually thunderstorms didn't last long, but when they were severe, we closed up the house, both doors and windows, until it was over. If they lasted a long time, then we would find inside work to do.

One night, Dad was in the house watching lightning strike close by along the river and a pain shot up his leg. The wide pine floorboards in the house had lots of nails, and he was standing on a nail.

The buildings weren't grounded, and sometimes in a severe thunderstorm Dad would turn the cows out into the barnyard. He said he could replace hay better than the cows. It didn't happen often, and usually at night, it seemed. The cows weren't bothered by the lightning, the noise, and the rain. They seemed to know when Dad showed up what they were expected to do, and they didn't hesitate.

Getting crops in the ground at an early date was important because selling them was a source of cash, and what the winter weather had been had a lot to do with when we could start planting. There was no point in planting in April or early May, no matter how nice the weather, unless the ground had warmed up enough for the seeds to germinate. Farmers would go by how cold the winter had been, how much snow had piled up, how long it had stayed on the ground, and how much work the sun had been doing.

It wasn't an exact science. When you grow up with it, you learn how to read the soil. Dad would just know when to start planting so the seeds would germinate and grow.

CHAPTER TEN

Bringing in the Hay

Hay was harvested all summer long, both ours and hay we harvested from other farms that didn't want the hay. It took the summer to fill the barn.

We hayed whenever the hay was ready. You could tell by looking for seeds on the tops. You wanted to cut the hay before the seeds were there. If it was harvested too late, it wouldn't be nutritious for the cows and horses. Sometimes we even hayed at night if the hay was ready.

You never harvested green hay, and you would never put green hay in the barn. Green hay was moist, and when it dried, there was a chemical reaction that caused heat. No problem outside in the open air, but inside a barn where there was no air flow, having green hay inside risked its heating up as it dried and causing a fire. That was the farmer's worst nightmare. Once the hay was ripe, Dad would gauge the weather for a stretch of dry days, because the cut hay would need a full day of sun to dry out. Then we'd get to it. The first day, we cut it. The next, we raked it into windrows while it dried. The third day, we pitchforked it onto the hay rack and towed it into the barn to build the mows. When the boys were no longer available, Susie and Sylvia would help.

When we had both horses, they'd be hooked up to the hay rack using a whiffletree to distribute the weight between them. When we were down to one horse, and Dad had built the tractor, we'd use the truck to tow the hay rack. I learned to drive the truck to load hay when I was 11 or 12 (didn't need a license to do that).

Once the hay rack full of loose hay was in the barn, we'd first pitchfork the hay off by hand to start

A whiffletree is a pivoted swinging bar to which the traces of the horse harnesses are fastened and at the midpoint of which the load to be towed is attached.

51

building the mow. Then we'd put the barn hay fork to work. The hay fork was like a giant grapple or tongs (except it had a row of tines on both sides) hanging down on a rope from a pulley that was up near the barn roof. The rope went the other way from the pulley to a horse and was connected to its harness. The hay fork would be let down onto the hay rack, and I would set its tines into the loose hay. Then, as Susie would lead the horse out of the barn, the tines would lock onto their load of hay and lift it up out of the hay rack. Once it was in the air, Dad could move it to where he wanted the load dumped and snap open the lock to release the hay.

We filled all the space available in the barn, right up to the roof (or as close as we could get to it). Most of the left side of the barn was open, except for a room at the front where the cow grain—a mixture of oats and corn—was stored, so you could start at the floor and build on up. On the right side, there were walls around, and a roof over the linters, so the mow on that side started about eight feet up. There were two scaffolds reaching from one side to the other about halfway to the roof, so when the mow reached that height, it extended from one side of the barn to the other.

Bringing in the hay.

Scaffolding in the barn.

Dad himself was the only person allowed up in the barn to guide the hay fork up over the scaffolds and unlock them. It was risky business—Horace Allen had been hurt bad by a falling hay fork—and Dad thought he was the only one who should do it. It was very hot, as well, up there at the top of the barn and he didn't mind the heat.

I always wore shorts when we were haying, which Dad said was a dumb idea. At the end of a hot day of haying, I'd be covered with chaff from the hay, and I always hoped the tide would be up so we could take a quick swim in the river. We'd go in off the ledge at the end of our point.

We never had a mice problem in the barn, despite all the grain storage, and the reason was our farm cats, who lived in the hay year-round. They would burrow into the hay to have their kittens, and

We didn't go in the river for more than enough to rinse off the chaff. The mills upstream had dumped so much stuff in the river, it wasn't healthy, but boy, did that cool water feel good!

it was a race between Dad and me to find them. He wanted to keep the population down. I saw no need to. One year, I counted seventeen cats and kittens living in our barn.

CHAPTER ELEVEN

Family and Schooling

George Jr., Ruth, and Roberta.

When I was little, there were five of us. My sister Ruth was 16 when I was born, and she was upset with my mother for having another baby. She said she was tired of helping take care of boys, and would only forgive her if I was a girl. My oldest brother, Harold, was 15, my middle brother, Gilbert, was 10, and my youngest brother, George, was seven, so I really grew up alone from the time I was 10.

My sister was married when I was three, and she took me to visit her a lot. She bought me a doll when I was four that was as big as I was, as well as doll clothes, a stove, small chairs, etc. My Dad built a table to go with the chairs so I could have a doll "party." My cousin Pelham Howe and I were the same age, so he used to come spend the day with me.

While my mother did her work, I played with my dolls. When she had time, she crocheted baby sets to ship to Boston to sell. She taught me to crochet when I was four or five, and I had a little red rocking chair that I sat in right beside her as she worked. We listened to "soaps" on the radio.

When I was not quite 4½ years old, I had an accident and got burned, bad. Dad and my brother Harold had been working in the woods when Harold cut his leg, and they came back to the house to take care of it. My brother George and I were standing by the stove, and when I saw Harold bleeding, I suddenly felt funny and fainted dead away. We had a half-grown dog that had a basket behind the stove with a handle that was against the back of the stove. I landed on the handle and burned my neck, forehead, and nose.

It was midwinter and was storming, and the doctor was in Wiscasset a half hour away, and Harold, with his patched-up leg, drove my Mom and me there. The doctor said the burn was deep and close to the artery. I guess I was lucky, but healing took a long time, and I was unhappy. I had bad earaches and Dad would blow pipe smoke in my ears, which made them feel better. He listened to the radio in the evening, and I would sit on his lap and often go to sleep. Since I was already in my pj's, he would put me in bed.

I started first grade the week after I turned seven. I could have started the year before, but there were Gypsies camped in the neighborhood, and Dad didn't want his six-year-old daughter walking the two miles each way to school past the field where they were tented. He couldn't take me because he had to milk the cows. George had just finished the eighth grade, and he would ride me to school on his bicycle.

The school was by the Four Corners on the River Road on the road down to the Chops on the river. There was another school not so far away, but it had been consolidated into ours.

We had one room and one teacher, Florence Temple, for the eight grades and twenty-five pupils. She was in her thirties and had two kids of her own in the school, a girl a couple of years older than me, and a boy a year or so younger. She did everything at the school, from opening the door in the morning and stoking the woodstove, to teaching the three R's, to being the janitor when the 8:30 to 3:30 school day was over and the kids had gone home. In winter, it would still be cold inside when we arrived in the morning, and everyone would draw their chairs close to the woodstove until it heated up.

Miss Temple separated us into three groups, first and second grades, third and fourth grades, and then the rest. Each group had its assignments, and she would bring each group down separately to the front of the room near the stove while she went over our lessons with us. There was a blackboard we used that ran the whole width of the room.

Each group was supposed to tend to its own lessons when another group was in the front with her—but us younger kids would listen to the lessons for the older kids, and we'd know those lessons when it came our turn to be the older group.

Our woodstove was a round potbelly stove, and there was a board hung above it for our boots when they needed to be dried.

There was no plumbing. Every day a couple of us would be delegated to carry jugs over to a private house across the Four Corners to get drinking water. That was a good distance, too. There were two privies—one boys, one girls—they were both two-holers and went to the same place. To make a little cash, Dad cleared out the privies at the end of the school year. He also sold to the town the wood needed for the woodstove.

From first grade on, after chores, I walked the two miles to school, and back again, every day. Winter was no different, unless there was a blizzard and the radio would tell us the school was closed. Dad told me to wear a scarf, and I did. It was a lot colder in the winter then, and sometimes it would be minus 20 degrees for days, but I walked with a scarf tied around my face.

Miss Temple was dedicated, and amazing. Everyone liked her and respected her, even the bullies. But after eight years with her, I had to go on, to high school in Bath. It wasn't easy. In order to go to high school, I had to find transportation or live around. At first, I rode with Clyde Perkins, one of the neighbors who worked at Bath Iron Works. I met him at the head of our road at 5:30 a.m., and he dropped me off at the Bath Post Office, which meant I had to wait there until 7:45 to walk up the hill to Morse High. Then at night I had to wait until about 4:30, after his workday, to go home. Long day.

For the rest of that year, I stayed with my great-uncle John Howe in upper Bath and went home weekends, to help at the farm.

It was an unhappy time for me, for many reasons, and I quit school that first year. Both my Dad and my Mom were disappointed, my Mom especially. My Dad never said anything, just asked me that summer if I was going back? I thought about it a long time, and then told him I was. I had then, and have ever had, a desire to learn. It was important to my Mom that I graduate high school, as Ruth had done—but not my brothers—and it became important to me. I was determined I would finish high school.

The next year, I stayed with my brother George and his wife Betty at Sagadahoc Ferry, just on the Woolwich side of the Carlton Bridge. I had to walk the bridge every morning on the way to Morse High up the hill on High Street. The wind coming down the river whistled over the bridge, and there wasn't any protection from it, except on the middle section that raised up and down like an elevator for tall boats going under it. It was pretty cold in the middle of winter.

For the last year and a half, I stayed with Ruth and Jud, who worked at the Hyde Windlass Company. It was much easier even though I still had a long wait in the morning. There were about five of us from Woolwich who all waited together at the Bath Post Office till it was time to walk up the hill to school. We were allowed to hang out there, so long as we made no trouble, so that early morning time with them was like heaven for me.

I wasn't exactly a social butterfly, and when I graduated, there was no one to take me to the senior dance. Hearing that, my brother Gilbert came home from California for it and took me. My sister made a beautiful dress for me to wear. I felt special. Gil and I danced the "real" dances at the senior dance, unlike most who didn't know how, and I was a very happy girl.

With all that said, I was not home much to help my father while in high school. I was determined to graduate, and he insisted I should do it, but it meant he had to do the chores by himself, as both Harold and George had jobs. Mom helped as much as she could, but it was hard on him.

I decided after high school not to leave again and not have any help for Dad at the farm, so I stayed on to work with him and chose not to go to college then (I went later, in my thirties). I couldn't leave my Dad to do all of the work by himself. I stayed on at the farm, and after I got married, Vic and I lived there in the "other part" of the house until Dad had to sell the cattle.

CHAPTER TWELVE

The Importance of Hunting

We had to fend for ourselves, and hunting was a necessary part of our lives. We were familiar with guns, how to handle them, how to shoot them, and what to do with the kill. We hunted some for sport, but mostly for food—deer, ducks, upland birds (partridges and pheasants), and rabbits. I started going with Dad deer hunting when I was about 12 years old, but carried no gun. I'm sure he lost a lot of chances for getting a deer with me around, but it was better for me to learn how to walk in the woods doing it that way.

Dad was a crack shot. He once shot a deer at 300 yards. It was a slightly uphill shot, and if you are shooting either up or downhill, you have to adjust your shot to compensate for the rise or fall of the bullet. It was late in the day, too. He couldn't believe he killed it until he found it. Most of his deer were a lot closer than that.

I was pretty good, too. Still am. The squirrels around where I live know that.

I didn't see that kill, but I know no one could outshoot him, and I know he was a great wing shot. I saw him shoot plenty of ducks in a fly-by out on the island in the cove. It's not easy to shoot ducks flying by at full speed. You have to know just how far to lead them.

Dad had a Remington 12-gauge pump gun, a .30-30 carbine, a .30-06 long rifle, and a couple of .22 rifles that were kept on the gun rack. He had a .38 caliber handgun and my Mom had a stainless steel .32 caliber handgun. He'd inherited some, bought others. His favorite gun was the .30-30 carbine lever-action, which he used for deer hunting. I don't recall him using the handguns for anything except killing the pig, but he kept them clean and kept them in the gun cabinet.

There was a roller towel rack on the inside of the kitchen door that was five feet off the floor. Dad told us when our heads reached that, we could learn how to handle a gun and hunt. I reached it when I was about 15. My sister Ruth was never that tall, so she didn't qualify, but she didn't want to hunt, anyway.

We learned to shoot with both a .22 and a single-barrel 16-gauge shotgun. My middle brother, Gilbert, used to shoot gray squirrels with the .22, then skin and fry them. They taste like chicken, pretty good to eat.

We carried the shotgun empty until Dad was convinced we could handle it safely through fences and around trees, especially in snow. He was a patient man. When he knew I was ready, I started to carry a single-shot .22. We didn't need a license until we were 16 years old, but had to be with a parent or guardian. My oldest brother let me use his .22 long rifle and I shot my first deer with it. With a .22, you had to shoot him in the head; otherwise, you'd just wound him.

We hunted on our own land, on the land behind the back pasture, where the pond is, and on the land behind the back pasture toward Route 127 that was owned then by Carroll Perkins's Uncle George, who gave us permission to hunt there. That's how it was then in Woolwich. You either hunted your own land, or by permission. If you wanted to hunt on someone else's land, you asked for permission. No one saw a need to post their land.

That changed one year when a bunch of guys without permission began regularly going through our woods in the morning before we could get out. By the time we got out hunting, the deer had been driven away. Dad posted the land as a result. We posted the home and middle pastures, and Dad signed every one of the signs to make sure they were legal.

One day we were hunting and had gone to the house for lunch. When we got back to the main road and were deciding where we were going next, a guy with a gun came along and walked right past us, maybe six of us with guns, and started to go into the woods. Dad asked him who gave him permission to hunt there. He said he didn't need permission. Dad said he did, told him the land was his and he didn't

Gilbert with the deer he shot on his first hunt after getting out of the Air Force.

have permission to hunt there. The guy asked what he was going to do about it and kept on going. My brother said, "Boy, you got to have a lot of balls to walk past the owner and six guns and no trespassing signs." That didn't stop him either.

Dad didn't want me to go in the woods by myself after that.

Deer season was November, and Dad went out by himself as often as he could, but he had to take the milk to the dairy first. After I got my driver's license, I would take the milk so he could go out. He usually got a deer, and usually toward the end of November. It was cold enough then for the meat to keep.

My brother Gil was also a terrific hunter, and when he came home from the Air Force after the war, he went out on our November hunts. And he was successful.

My brother Harold worked evenings, so he would go by himself during the days, but on most Saturdays the family went out together. The hunting party would be family, my sister Ruth's husband, Jud,

Sylvia with her first deer.

and Carroll, Susie, and Sylvia Perkins. Once in a while, a friend of my brother George's would go with us. Everyone went hunting together on Thanksgiving Day, and then we'd all have dinner together.

Susie, Sylvia, and I were the ones who walked through the woods hoping to scare out a deer or two toward those waiting around the edges. Sometimes a deer would be spooked by one of us, and that's what happened when the deer I shot with the .22 came toward me from where Susie was walking. We "surprised" each other, and she wasn't far from me when I shot her. I knew she needed to be shot in the head, and it was possible because she stopped just long enough for me to take a good aim at her. She was about 80–85 pounds.

Not all our deer came out of the hunt. Sylvia shot her first deer because it made the mistake of trespassing on both our land and hers. That was quite a chase. He swam across the river from Swan Island to our shore, went through the woods and down behind Sylvia's house, heading toward the river. Sylvia shot him just before he got to the riverbank.

My Dad was hunting alone one day and shot a deer. It was quite a distance to get it out to the woods road, and he was wondering how it was going to be done as he walked toward it. When he got within 25 or 30 feet of it, it jumped up and ran away. Dad was so surprised he could only stand and watch it go.

The last deer he shot was a buck with a nice set of antlers. He had the head preserved, and it hung over my fireplace mantel years later while he lived with us.

After a deer was shot, it was gutted and field-dressed in the woods. (Dad would keep the liver for dinner.) The deer carcass was hung in the shed with the skin on until Dad skinned it and cut it in quarters. He knew how to butcher. It stayed cold enough in November for it to keep well, so it hung there as long as it was cold. Most of the rump meat was eaten as steak. Then the rest was cut up and used for other things. The neck and rib meat went into mincemeat, which was canned. Since we didn't have electricity, the meat for mincemeat had to be "hand ground." That built muscles—and that was my job. If you like mincemeat, deer mincemeat is the best.

What was canned was the shoulder meat that wasn't eaten as steak. Dad cut the meat from the bones and Mom cut it into the size she wanted for stew meat and canning. The stew meat was cooked before canning and was used for stew when the jars were opened.

Sometimes the hide was taken to a place in Hallowell to be processed into leather and sometimes it was just buried along with the head and legs. Deer-hide leather is warm even without lining, and there was a woman who would make some of it into gloves or mittens. She'd also take some of the rabbit skins. I think she used the fur for lining the gloves and mittens.

There weren't many wardens around back then, and they stayed in an area for longer periods, so we knew them. One I remember was Bill Gordon, a good guy. We were all out together one day when he came by. He just reminded us that there was only supposed to be five in the party.

Percy Nelder was another. He was the one who told Dad not to be concerned if he happened to hit a goose while trying to drive them away, and he used to stop by occasionally to talk, but not for anything to eat. One time, Walter Baker, another farmer and friend of Dad's he played checkers with, shot a deer after the season was over and was sitting on it to rest when Percy came by. Percy told him to be careful crossing the road, and went about his business.

Farmers were favored by the wardens, I think. They knew we weren't hunting just for sport.

———————

CHAPTER THIRTEEN

Duck and Bird Hunting

The first thing we hunted in the fall were ducks and geese. The daily limit for ducks then was four, so each of us could get four. And we did. Quite a few of the ducks were teal, which are small, so it takes four to make a meal. The possession limit for geese was two per hunter. One goose made a good meal, and, after plucking them, we used their down in pillows, either bed pillows or fancy pillows for a couch.

We hunted ducks in two places. Out front of the farm in the river is a small piece of land (it's shown on the river maps as "Ames ledge"). It belonged to us because you can own to low-water line, and we could walk out to this piece of land when the tide was out. The ducks came right over it from Merrymeeting Bay after they were shot at down there.

Dad had built a "gunning" boat big enough for two people that was only used for duck and goose hunting on the river. It had a hole in the

Dad in his "gunning" boat.

rear transom for the sculling oar. The bow was decorated with grass and hay to hide the boat from the ducks and geese. My Dad was an expert at sculling up to a bunch of ducks before they saw us. He stored the gunning boat the rest of the year in the brick Coast Guard building.

When the ducks flew up from the Bay, they would land in any water they could find, and we also used to hunt ducks by a small pond way up in the back pasture. Dad had a blond cocker spaniel that loved to hunt with him and go fetch the ducks to him. They used to go up to the pond and get a couple of ducks. Dad had made a blind up there, and the dog would wait with him in the blind to go fetch the ducks.

Dad also took his cocker to hunt upland birds—woodcock, partridge, and pheasants. (Woodcock and partridge were wild, but the pheasants were raised in captivity and released.) You had to be quick, because they jumped fast when flushed and would be gone before you could get the gun ready. Sometimes we would flush them when deer hunting, but we'd be carrying a rifle and just had to watch. Wrong kind of ammunition.

The meat from wild birds tastes like no other meat and is hard to describe, except it is "wild"-tasting, whatever that means. Mom soaked them overnight in salt water to reduce their wild flavor. Then they could be roasted or baked in the oven like any other bird. No need to season them after being soaked in salt water. Some people say geese are fatty, but that's domestic geese that don't fly. Canada geese are all dark meat, darker than other wild birds, so their flavor is stronger.

Mom used to cover goose breasts with sliced bacon to keep them from drying out.

There was another kind of bird hunting my Dad did that we didn't talk about. In the springtime, Canada geese would come into the fields for the nice green grass that was going to become part of our hay for the winter. It seemed as if there were hundreds of them, and they would pull the grass up by the roots so it would have to be reseeded. Those geese were protected then, so Dad asked the warden what could be done about them. The warden told him he should shoot a gun over their heads and scare them away, and if he happened to hit one, not to be concerned about it.

Despite their long flight from the south, the geese were plump after they'd eaten our grass for a while. Even though the warden had told us it was okay, we were very cautious about who saw us killing and eating one. We would rush out into the field to bring the goose inside and into a small cool space under the kitchen where we kept it until we plucked it. (There was a small trapdoor in the kitchen that opened into that space.)

Mom would make me a goose sandwich for my lunch, and Dad said that if anyone asked me what it was, I was to tell them it was "meat." If my girlfriend came to visit, I had to keep her out of the kitchen and dining room.

———⟫●⟪———

CHAPTER FOURTEEN

The Pig

Dad got a piglet every spring from a pig farm in Whitefield (I think it's still there), usually about six weeks or two months old when he got it. It was my job to take care of it and feed and water it and raise it until it was time to slaughter it. The pig lived outside in a pen under the stable where the horses were, and I fed it through a space left open for that purpose.

When the pig was small, I fed it corn mash mixed with warm water and some milk. As it grew, the mash was fed dry with scraps of leftover food mixed with it, and plenty of water. The pig ate everything I gave it.

I also scratched its back—to hear it squeal—and talked to it.

I knew what its fate was, but that was my job.

Contrary to what people believe, pigs aren't messy and they don't smell. Pigs are the easiest animals to raise. You just keep them in small quarters, so they will keep the fat on, and don't let them run free. My grandmother (Dad's mother) had a pig that slept behind the woodstove until she thought it was warm enough to put it outside. It was surprising how neat it was in the house. She took it outdoors to go to the bathroom.

We had one every year, and after I'd fed it and watered it and raised it, it grew it to be 250–300 pounds before Dad killed it late in the fall and took it to our relatives, the Eameses, in Richmond, for processing.

I used to hide that day. There was no squealing because Dad shot it in the head with his handgun, but it was a hard day for me.

He gutted it and cut it in quarters to take to Eames to be processed into bacon, chops, roasts, etc. He had boiling water handy to soften the stiff bristles so that he could shave them off. He didn't want the bristles for anything but just wanted to have the skin clear and ready to process. He had a special, sharp straight razor for that purpose. The pig's quarters with the skin shaved was the finished product on our end.

There was a room in the basement in the front part of the house where it was cool. That room was reserved for food that wasn't canned, like meat, pork, sauerkraut, etc. After we got the processed pig back from Eames, the meat was hung up in there and would keep.

We got salt pork from the pig that we ate with baked beans and brown bread. Baked beans every Saturday night.

———◆———

CHAPTER FIFTEEN

Feeding the Family

Our kitchen faced the barn and was probably 20 feet long, with the cookstove on the end near the living room and the shed and stable on the other end. Opposite the kitchen and facing the driveway was, first of all, the dining room, and then, at the shed end, the pantry, where Mom did her food preparation. The icebox was in the pantry, and there was a door between the pantry and the kitchen that was hardly ever closed in summer. It was only kept closed in winter when it was really cold and Mom had to do her food prep in the kitchen.

The cookstove was one of the two stoves that heated the house in winter, and it was kept going all day. It had a water tank on the left side that stayed warm all the time. We always kept a pail of water,

Even on hot days in summer, the stove was going most of the day, just for cooking.

which we used for one thing or another, on a shelf by the door to the shed. On winter mornings, after a real cold night when the stove had gone out, the top of the water in the pail would be ice.

The pantry had cabinets on the wall next to the shed, and underneath one of them was a wooden barrel with a lid where Mom kept a 50-pound bag of flour, along with a 30-pound bag of sugar. (She bought salt in five-pound bags.) We bought the flour and sugar from the same place we bought bags of grain for the cattle, which we did every couple of weeks.

When I first went with Dad to get the grain, it came from a grain company in Wiscasset down toward the water from where Red's Eats now is. Later, after the grain company went out of business,

The grain came in bags made of cloth that was very good material. During the war, Mom used to make dresses and aprons out of it, and other things.

we picked up the grain in West Bath from a railroad car left for that purpose by the railroad on a side track.

> Dad wanted biscuits at every meal, and that was our bread. Mom didn't make regular bread, except for brown bread, which was unleavened, and which we always had with baked beans.

There were shelves on the pantry wall next to the dining room, and a big shelf on the other wall by the door into the kitchen. That shelf was Mom's work space where she did her prep work and rolled out her pie crusts. There also were small shelves over that work space where the spices were kept. (Sometimes she'd use a little spice, like nutmeg or cinnamon, but not much.) The pantry wall next to the shed was cold in winter, which was good for keeping some of the food, not so good for preparing the food. When it got real cold, she would have to do that part on a table in the kitchen.

Mom's cooking was regular and straightforward, nothing fancy—but she knew how to cook, and she fed us three full meals every day.

All the women in the family liked to cook, me included, and watching my Mom cook fascinated me. She started out using my Grandmother Ames's handwritten cookbook, but by the time I was around, she didn't need the book. She knew all the recipes, including the two shown here.

MOTHER AMES' MOLASSES CAKE
3/4 cup sugar
1/4 cup lard
1/4 cup molasses
1 tsp. soda
1 egg
3/4 cup buttermilk
1 3/4 cup flour
1/2 tsp. each of cassia* and clove (substitute cinnamon)

JOHNNIE CAKE
2/3 cup corn meal
2 cups flour
1 1/2 tsp. soda
Pinch salt
2 mixing spoons sugar
Mixing spoon sour cream
1 egg
About 1 1/2 buttermilk

---

*Cassia is a spice that isn't used anymore, but cinnamon can be used instead.

Neither of these recipes showed a cooking temperature or time, probably because there was a lot of variation between ovens, and every cook needed to know how her own oven baked. I would use a 350° oven for 35–40 minutes, testing the cake after 30 minutes.

Cooking was in my genes, I think. For me, it was about creating something. One day while Mom was crocheting—I was probably 10—I went into the pantry looking through my grandmother's cookbook, found a recipe for cookies, and decided to see if I could make them. Mom asked what I was doing, and of course I said, "Nothing," but I made some spice cookies that turned out really well. I gave some to my grandmother's husband, and he liked them very much. Naturally I made them for him often. Cooking has been important to me my whole life.

> For ten years during tourist season (May 1 through Columbus Day), I was the pastry cook at County Fair, a restaurant on Main Street in Damariscotta. I made specialty cakes at home all year—wedding cakes, birthday cakes, etc. Dad used to like to watch me decorate the cakes. "Looks almost like plastering,'" he said.

Mom made doughnuts every Saturday morning, and whoever was there lined up to get the doughnut "holes." Breakfast was usually eggs, bacon, fried potatoes, and biscuits, all except the biscuits done on the cookstove top. She used bacon fat for frying and for shortening for the biscuits, and always kept some in a container on the stove top so it wouldn't get hard.

The biscuits were made of flour and soda and cream of tartar, and just enough milk so you could roll it out. She used tin cookie sheets to bake the biscuits on so you could make twelve or fifteen biscuits at a time, about an inch thick before they were baked, and 2 to 2½ inches thick afterward. When everyone was home, she made biscuits every day.

We made and used a lot of butter, and sold some. There was always butter on the table. When we were making it by hand, we'd have some milk in a container and wait until it started to sour, which is when cream separates from the milk. Then you churn the separated cream in a bowl until you have butter. (It was always hard to get all the milk out of the butter.) Dad later got Mom a big glass jar with a crank outside and a paddle inside attached to a screw-on top. You cranked it until the paddle made butter.

The milk that had been separated out was skim milk, and Mom used it in cooking. My brother George liked skim milk, so she would save some for him.

There wasn't much difference between the midday meal and supper. Each one was whatever meat was on hand, plus potatoes, one or more vegetables, and dessert. No one was picky about the menu. We ate whatever Mom decided to cook for us. We had deer meat, either fresh or canned to preserve it, or pork that had been smoked by the Eameses in Richmond. Rabbit if the boys had been lucky. Duck during hunting season. You could only take four ducks a day per person, and that was hardly enough to go around, so we had duck whenever they were shot, and didn't try to preserve them in any way.

Occasionally Dad would buy a roast, or some liver, which he really liked and which couldn't be preserved. In the wintertime, if Dad wanted to have eel for dinner, he would cut a hole in the ice in the cove, about halfway to Hathorn's in the shallows, put something down the hole and come back with an eel or two. He could catch one whenever he wanted. Some were big, three to four feet long, and there were plenty of them in the cove. Mom didn't like frying them because even dead two days and with heads cut off, they would wiggle in the pan.

When the boys had had a good day smelting in winter, we'd have a mess of fried smelts, and the boys even helped with the frying! It took a lot of smelts to feed us a meal. Except for smelts, we didn't eat fish from the river. It was already beginning to be polluted from the mills upstream. Smelts came straight from their spawning grounds and were no problem.

On a special day, Thanksgiving or Christmas or Easter, Mom would roast one of the geese she'd been raising, after killing and plucking it, saving its down for pillows or quilts, and cleaning out its innards.

Our vegetables would come from what we had grown and stored. We had bins of beets, potatoes, and carrots in the cellar under the front part of the house, and they kept well there. Turnips and cabbage were kept in the underground cellar over at Thwings, but most of those were kept for sale.

Dessert was special, and we had dessert every day, at both big meals. Mom baked pies and cakes with whatever was in season that we'd picked—apples, blueberries, rhubarb from our great 150-year-old rhubarb patch, chocolate cream pie, or simple custard made with milk, eggs, and sugar. We had rice pudding, tapioca pudding, chocolate pudding, or bread pudding made in the oven, whatever Mom wanted to make. If there wasn't anything else, she would make cookies for us.

When she made pies, she'd make four at a time and keep the extras in the pantry. They didn't last long.

We had an oak dining table with three leaves and eight chairs. The table was square without any leaves in it, but it usually had one, and all three when everybody was there or we had company. The table and the chairs had been there for more years than my parents had. Dad sat toward the end of the side facing the driveway, and Mom sat at the end of the table, to his right.

The food was served family style in serving dishes on the table, and my father served us. We could have seconds if we wanted them, but the "firsts" were what my father thought was enough for our sex and age. No food was wasted. We had hash made with the last of roasts and fish along with vegetables. Soups and stews were made a lot and served at supper.

The cookstove was always stoked and always working.

We had no trouble with mice or ants, inside the house or out. The cats took care of them. Had no problem with other critters, either. They seemed to stay away. I think maybe the cats scared them off.

I was amazed then, and am amazed now, how Mom could do everything she did and still find time to make clothes for us, to knit and to sew, and to make clothes—bed jackets—for sale. She was remarkable, and I always wanted to make her proud.

———⟶➤●◄⟵———

CHAPTER SIXTEEN

Winters

Winters on the farm were hard.

The harvesting and marketing of cash crops for sale, and for ourselves, and preserving them, the cutting of fields and harvesting hay of summer, and filling the barn and the stable with hay for the cows and the horses—all that was traded into shoveling and plowing snow for the winter, harvesting the ice, and filling the ice stack.

And getting ready for spring.

Winters started earlier, then. We usually had snow in November, and it would snow most of the winter, right through March. There was a lot of shoveling to do, with the barn being 200 feet from the house and the milk house being 75 feet from the barn. We shoveled a path three or four feet wide straight from the house to the milk house and from there to the cattle door on the side of the barn behind the cows, and then to the pump house from which the water for the cows came. (The big barn door toward the river was only used for haying and for grain delivery, etc.) The driveway leading from the stable to the roadway, where the car was kept, also needed shoveling.

We didn't have a snowplow for the truck. Dad had a plow that the horses pulled around the house to the barn to keep the roadway clear, but we relied on the Town tractor to come in and clear our road. Even though Dad was the Road Commissioner, that often didn't happen until late morning, and we had to get the milk to the dairy in Bath. Usually we did. If we couldn't get out to take the milk to the dairy we took it all the next day.

In the storm of February 1952, we were snowed in for three days because there was so much snow, it piled up, and then it kept drifting from the wind. Everything we had was full of milk. We might have been snowed in, but the cows still had to be milked. We were awash in milk, and by the time we could get out to take it to the dairy, it took two trips to get it there.

We were still up at 4:30 a.m. Since we didn't have electricity we used two lanterns to light our way to the barn and around inside it. The lanterns were about 30 inches tall with a bail on top to hang them up by. The globe was heavy glass that was protected by two heavy wires that circled the glass. They held about a pint of oil and had to be cleaned and filled every day.

One lantern was hung behind the cows on each end of the row of cow stalls in the barn. It was dim but gave us enough light to see what we needed to see. Most of our work was repetitive, so it worked out just fine.

The cows' body heat kept the barn warm, warm enough we could take off our jackets while we were milking.

Once we got two large pails filled with milk, we carried them to the milk house, where there was a strainer. We strained the milk in the pails through cheesecloth directly into the large milk cans we took to the dairy. We filled two of those large cans each milking, twice a day.

The milk was supposed to be at the dairy by 10:30 a.m., so we took it after breakfast. For a time, we only took it up the hill to Horace Allen, who would take our milk to the dairy along with his. Years later, after Horace sold his cattle, we had to take our milk to the dairy ourselves. After I got my license, I was the one who took it.

The cows were kept in the barn from frost to green grass. We fed them their hay while it was still daylight so we didn't have to take lanterns into the part of the barn where the hay was. The cows were never out in the snow.

If it wasn't too cold, Dad would work in the shop in the stable, building and repairing the things we were going to need when planting season came around again.

Sometimes it would get really cold at night. When it reached minus 20 degrees or colder, Dad would go out to check on the cows,

The sawdust was there to sop up the cows' urine. It was especially uncomfortable for them in winter. Dad would sometimes make two or three visits a night to be sure they were comfortable. The wet sawdust got shoveled into the cellar along with the manure.

make sure they were clean, and put down extra sawdust for the night before he went to bed. The stable where the horses lived was a small space, and closed in, and their bodies were quite warm, so it didn't usually get very cold there. When it did, we had blankets for the horses.

He took very good care of his animals.

School was in session until 3:15 p.m., so by the time I got home, it was already dark, and I still had homework to do. Winter wasn't easy for studying, but we had two Aladdin lamps that were much brighter than the kerosene wick lamps, and that helped.

The major winter project was cutting firewood for the next year. Dad would take the horse and dog up to the middle pasture for the day. I would take his lunch to him on most days so he would have hot coffee or tea and sandwiches that weren't frozen. He left the wood cut and stacked in cordwood lengths to dry until the next fall. Then a gas-powered portable saw went around from farm to farm to cut the cordwood into woodstove lengths. After it was cut into stove wood, it was thrown into the truck and put into the shed. When next winter started, the shed was full to the top with nice dry stove wood.

Our cocker spaniel liked to sled on the snow. I would push him down the little hill from the house past the stable, and he would sit and wait for me to come tow him up the hill and do it over again. When I was little, I would sit on the sled with him.

We had three dogs, two cockers and a collie. The collie was my companion. One of the cockers belonged to Gil, but he left it with us when he went off to the war. The other cocker was Dad's bird dog.

Dad would go skating with or without us on the river. The tide would leave water on top of the ice and make the ice smooth out toward the middle of the river, so it was almost always good skating. When Sylvia got old enough, her mother, Susie, would bring her down and we would all go skating, except my mother, who didn't like skating.

Around mid-February, we'd start checking on the potatoes we'd stored in the underground cellar on the Thwings' place to see if their "eyes" were sprouting. They had to be cut into sections with an eye in each piece so we could use them for planting in the spring.

We had to plan for planting corn, too. We dried the corn on the ear, and the ears of corn were stored with the potatoes. The corn had to be taken off the ear to plant, and we had to keep the different kinds of corn separate.

When the maple trees down in the swamp began to wake up again in February and early March, and their sap began to run, we harvested it. We had taps hammered into the trees, and buckets hung from the taps to catch the sap. Gathering the sap from the buckets every day was my job, and there would still be snow on the ground, sometimes deep. Dad put a box big enough for two milk cans on the sled, I put on my snowshoes and went off, towing the sled. There was usually enough sap to fill both milk cans after I'd emptied the buckets into them.

Mom had two kettles on the stove to put the sap in. One was for the sap that was being "cooked down" and the other was for the fresh sap. They would be put together as the sap was boiled down and reduced into syrup. It took 40 quarts to make one quart of syrup. A lot of work went into that quart of syrup, but it was worth the effort when it was used on top of homemade pancakes or waffles.

We didn't sell maple syrup, but we gave some to family—Uncle John and Uncle Dave—and to the Perkinses. Our maple syrup was one of the things the aunts and uncles would come for on Sundays.

CHAPTER SEVENTEEN

Smelting on the Kennebec

One of the things we did in winter to put food on the table was go smelting on the river.

We smelted from inside fishing camps (we called them "camps," not "shacks"), which were about eight foot square. We built our own camps. They were frames with canvas stretched over them. The canvas was waterproofed with whitewash. There was a door and a hole for the stove to vent. There would be some small shelves in the corners for bait, blood worms, and matches, etc., for the stove. We sat on boxes with open fronts, and we kept the smelts in there.

On the side opposite the door, the floor of the camp was open for about 12 or 14 inches, and a long hole called a "race" was cut in the ice to match the opening. Ice would form in the hole, so it needed to be cleared at least every two to three days. There was a flexible cable over the race from which we hung fish lines with treble hooks at the ends. Blood worms were used as bait, but when the fish were running well, no bait was needed because they'd grab the hooks with or without bait. There were six lines in a single camp and twelve lines in a double camp. The double camp had boards between two races.

Canvas smelt camp on Sheepscot River ice, between 1904 and 1906.
Collections of the Maine State Museum (91.26.616)

When smelts got hooked, they ran with the line and would tangle the lines so we were kept busy taking them off the hooks, untangling the lines, and putting new bait on. It sounds like slow motion, but it kept two people very busy while the fish were coming in with the tide.

The "stove" would be one of our big milk cans, which was about four feet tall. The cans were cut just below the handles, and I don't remember what was used to replace the can tops. A hole was cut in the lower part of the can for a draft to keep the fire burning. We used hardwood blocks for the fire so it wouldn't burn too fast. The stove gave off plenty of heat so we could remove our jackets while in the camp. It would get pretty warm, even at minus 20. It was a lot of fun when the smelts were biting well but pretty boring when they weren't.

My brother Gilbert had a camp off the Dresden shore one year and left it out too long. One day, Dad looked out on the river and saw Gil's camp floating downriver on a patch of ice. Gil wanted to save it, but it was too risky, and Dad talked him out of it.

My brothers had camps on the river on the west side by Brown's Point in Bowdoinham. That's where the channel is, and they would stay there and fish the tide, which is six hours. They caught a lot of smelt, sometimes as much as a hundred pounds in two tides. It was rare to catch that much, but there was a market for them in Bath and my brothers delivered them when they were fresh.

The smelts started to run in November and were usually done by the end of February. They were more plentiful toward spring, but leaving the camps on the river then was risky as the ice got thinner and the tides got stronger.

People who've never eaten smelts have missed a good treat. We prepared them by first slitting them and cutting off their heads. When you got the knack of it, the entrails would come out with the head when the head came off. Fry them in an iron frying pan with plenty of butter. Fried smelts are flavorful and taste like no other fish, sort of sweet compared to other fish.

Smelts and warm homemade biscuits made a good tasty lunch, but it took eight to ten six- to eight-inch smelts to make a meal, according to my appetite. In those days, there were six of us at home, and when we had a mess of smelts for dinner, there weren't any leftovers.

I was seven years younger than my next older brother, and when I asked to go along with them smelting, they said there wasn't enough room in the camp. I learned later there was only room for two in the camp, and both had to be fishing. At the time, though, I figured they just didn't want their kid sister tagging along after them. Also, they would have had to pull me on a sled because the snow was too deep for me to walk through.

So I had to wait until they were full grown and out of the house (two of them served in the Air Force during World War II) before I got to go smelting. Most of my smelt fishing was done on Great Salt Bay near Nobleboro after my husband Vic and I moved there. I used to go out smelt fishing by myself sometimes during the day when I was off work. I have more patience than brains, so I could sit there and watch for the lines to move longer than most people could.

We had a cat that knew when we were going fishing and would meet us at the door when we came in from the Bay. I usually gave her the last smelt we caught, and it would still be moving. She didn't eat it, of course, but just played with it.

I also did some freshwater smelting in the brooks in the spring, where you could just net them, but the Feds were afraid of overfishing so they stopped the netting. You could also catch them with your bare hands in the brooks, but the Feds said it was damaging to the fish if they were squeezed and not caught, so that was stopped, too. I think too many restrictions turned people off, so I'm not sure who fishes smelts anymore. I know there are some camps on the Kennebec in Dresden in the winter, if the ice freezes thick enough, but I don't know how they do.

Most of the smelts in the stores now come from Canada. I won't buy them because their heads are cut off and you can't tell how fresh they are. You can tell the freshness of smelts by their eyes, but not if their heads are cut off. It was different when I was being raised beside the Kennebec and my brothers were bringing in smelts. We knew how fresh they were.

——⟫●⟪——

CHAPTER EIGHTEEN

The Ice Stack

We didn't have electricity and didn't have refrigeration, but we needed ice for the dairy operation—the milk had to be kept cool—and we needed ice for our icebox, to keep our own milk and our meat and vegetables. We got ice the same way Ameses had gotten it for 150 years— from the river. We did it around late February, early March, when the ice was thickest, and before it began to melt. Sometimes we got the ice from the river in front of the house and sometimes we got it from the cove behind the Thwing house. It depended on the quality of the ice. The ice had to be solid and clear to keep well in the ice stack.

The ice stack was a separate building behind the barn on the river end. It was a four-sided upright about 30′ x 30′ and the height of the barn, with an open top. When full, it held about twenty tons of ice in 30″ x 30″ blocks. Dad had hauled tons of sawdust from the mills and piled it up over the summer and fall to put between layers of ice, to bank them and cover the open top after all the ice was in. The ice stayed frozen from one winter to the next.

Before electricity and refrigeration had come down the River Road, everybody had an icehouse that needed to be filled from the river. It was a community effort. Many of the older people in those families, like my grandfather, had worked in the ice trade and the families still had their tools, and used them. My Dad did.

Even after most people no longer had their own icehouses, friends and neighbors—the Perkinses, Reeds, and Allens—came and helped with getting our ice, just as Dad had helped them before they had refrigeration. Everyone helped each other on all kinds of work, not just ice harvesting. No one was "hired." No one expected to be paid.

If you needed them, they would come. If they needed you, you went.

Depending on people's availability, it took two or three weeks to harvest the ice needed to fill our ice stack.

We didn't have to clear a field on the ice because the river was tidal. The tide would flow over the ice and snow and turn the snow cover into ice. But we did have to mark out a field on the ice and chop a hole in the ice to start a channel. Once cut, blocks of ice would be led up the channel to a big wide sled that our horses pulled up over the fields to the ice stack.

The horses were critical. Dad had re-shod them with sharp caulks in their shoes, so they'd have traction on the roads and on the ice.

The channel would be marked by two lines from the hole, and the horses would straddle one line pulling a "groover" behind them, then the other line. The groover, guided like a plow, cut around four inches into the ice, and then the men would get to work with pries and ice saws. They had to break the blocks loose for them to be led up the channel to the sled. There they were picked out of the water and put on the sled for the horses to drag up to the ice stack. One sled-load, as I remember it, could hold enough ice for one ice layer in the ice stack.

Harvesting ice in Houlton, Maine, 1880–1890.
Courtesy of the Maine Historic Preservation Commission

Detail from painting, Cutting Ice on the Kennebec River at Dresden, ca. 1870. Collections of the Maine State Museum (2006.18.1)

A man would stand above an ice groove and saw up and down, using both hands. The saw teeth were not straight, but offset. That helped it cut easier. The ice was all cut by hand, and it was hard work. The only "payment" for the work was ice cream. We made ice cream every Sunday and in the summer sometimes two or three gallons; we needed ice and salt to make it. Friends, neighbors, and most of the family came and shared it. It had to be hand-churned.

As the ice blocks were put into the ice stack and a tier got filled up, they had to use a runner to slide the ice up to the next tier, and then a ramp as the tiers got higher. In the end, when they were close to the top, there'd be ice tongs around the block of ice, someone would be at the top pulling on a rope on the tongs, and someone would be below pushing. Every time a layer was filled up, sawdust would be shoveled around the sides to bank it, in between each row in the tier, and on top to get ready for the next tier.

The process was reversed when we took the ice out of the stack. Dad used ice tongs to move the ice around with, and either a sled or wheelbarrow to take it where it had to go. If it had to be cut, he cut it in the shed with an axe.

We had two iceboxes in the house, one in the main part, the other in the "other part." They were top loaders, and each had to have a drain attached to take care of the melt. The ice block had to be cut into about four pieces to fit into the space designated for it in the iceboxes. In warm weather, when my grandmother was in her cottage on the Hathorn farm, Dad also took care of filling her icebox.

For the dairy operation, regulations required that the milk had to be kept cool and a certain distance from the barn until we took it to the dairy. The little building we called the milk house, between the house and barn, had a big tank filled with water and ice to keep the cans of milk cool. The ice used for the milk cooler had to be filled every day. After Dad had cut the blocks into whatever sizes he needed for the iceboxes, he always used the leftover pieces in the milk tank.

Ice was critical for our survival—in the dairy operation and our iceboxes—and in our life on the farm.

CHAPTER NINETEEN

Getting Together: Kin, Friends, and Neighbors

Our life wasn't all work and no play. There was quite a lot of play, and a lot of music.

Mom and Dad both played the cornet and in the summer would go out on the front lawn and play them together. They were good, and people across the river would gather on the shore to listen and applaud. We had a piano in the parlor that Mom would play. Dad played the harmonica. On Sunday night, whoever was home would gather in the parlor and play music and sing. Two of my brothers played guitar and one sang, as well. I didn't play an instrument but had a pretty good voice, as Dad and Mom both did. Sometimes friends of my brothers would come and join us. And sometimes my Dad would just sit and play his harmonica for all of us.

We grew up on the dance floor (Dad was a good dancer), and we all went to the Days Ferry dances on Saturday night. The dance hall—it's no longer there—was on the sharp turn on the River Road leaving Days Ferry. Dad used to take everybody. If I got tired, I'd go to sleep on the benches. (There were no babysitters in those days.) The dance hall wasn't heated, so in winter, five or six couples would alternate going farm to farm on Saturdays for cards and dancing. Pushed furniture up against the wall to make space. We had a four-foot-high Victrola that had to be wound up to play the records, which were kept in the bottom, underneath the turntable. I was in charge of winding it up.

There was Bingo at the school on Saturday nights, and the whole family would go. After the war, the whole family was me, but there were other kids there with their parents. The prizes were food, sugar, eggs, and homemade bread and donuts.

Weekends were the time to visit. There was no invitation. People just showed up, and we were expecting them. If they hadn't come, we'd be concerned something might be wrong. If six people showed up, it didn't take Mom long to whip up a meal of baked beans, waffles, pancakes, and maple syrup.

Lots of people came. Annie, Dad's four-years-older sister, came with her husband, Dave Henderson. The two of them were dairy farmers like us and had Henderson's Dairy Farm in Bath. Uncle Dave was from Nova Scotia, and I don't know how they met, but Uncle Dave was a great storyteller. We loved to listen to his tall tales about growing up in Nova Scotia.

The tides in Nova Scotia, he said, run a whole lot faster than they do here, and they can surprise you. There was a kid who used to follow Dave's gang around, and they would tease him by taking him out on the flats and leaving him to race the tide in. It wasn't that the story was so funny, but the way Dave told it was. Aunt Annie adored him and laughed at his stories, no matter how many times she'd heard them. She and Dad were a lot alike.

Dad's uncle John Howe, who grew up and lived on Chops Point, worked at Bath Iron Works until he was 82, and used to come with his wife while we were milking so he could have some warm milk to drink right from the cow. I thought that idea was terrible (milk needed to be cold for me), but he loved it.

Uncle John was my grandmother's brother and the youngest of four. He was a hell-raiser growing up, probably didn't have enough to do, and the way he told his stories from that time made you laugh. As a kid, he used to get his dad's rifle and do practice shooting at the river buoy out on the channel when his dad went to town. It was a long shot, and in a strong tide the buoy moved back and forth a lot, so he would shoot at it and then take the boat to go see where he'd hit it.

His dad had a smokehouse on the riverbank where he smoked herring in the spring. One day, for whatever reason, Uncle John decided to shoot at the smokehouse where the herring were hanging to dry. When his dad came home and checked on the fish, he found them on the floor full of holes from Uncle John's target practice.

The way in which he and Dave told their stories is what made them funny. When we had the two of them together talking about when they were kids, we didn't need any other kind of entertainment.

But John raised his own kids right. His son became CEO of Bath Savings for 30 years, and his daughter became Superintendent of Schools in Yarmouth.

Carroll and Susie Perkins and their daughter Sylvia, from near the head of our road, always came. Carroll worked for a man in Day's Ferry who was a diver and repaired pier pilings. Carroll maintained his equipment. Susie and Sylvia worked on the farm with us, planting and weeding and winnowing the chaff from the grain. They dug potatoes with us and hayed with us. In the winter they went skating with us on the river.

Orrin Perkins, Carroll's uncle and one of Dad's oldest and best friends, lived in the brick house on the River Road, just across the Dresden line, a couple of houses south of his brother Gus, Carroll's Dad. He was a bachelor and came for dinner most nights, walking down the old Colonial rangeway road across the bog to us. Orrin was a true-blue Democrat in every way, and he would try to get Dad to talk politics. Dad was a registered Republican, but as far as he was concerned, friendship and politics weren't connected, and he didn't want them to be. He was expert at diverting the conversation on to other topics.

They would play checkers, and Dad would drive Orrin home after dark.

Gus was our best neighbor. He owned a manure spreader and brought his horse and wagon and manure spreader down every spring to help clear out the manure from our barn cellar and spread it on the fields and plowed ground. A lot of work.

There was Horace Allen, who owned the Reed house at the top of the hill, and whose mother was a Reed. We were kin with the Reeds, second or third cousins. He was a dairy farmer like us, had a big barn between his house and Carroll and Susie, had as many cows as us, and sold his milk to the same dairy. Big farm. They had electricity. He would take our milk to the dairy along with his, until he got hurt by falling hay tongs in his barn. Couldn't do much after that to tend his cattle and had to sell them.

Dad's friend Ed Jaquith, who introduced him to Mom, and his wife, Ella, would come up from Bath to visit and stay over Saturday night in the spare room. Ella and Mom had a good time together.

The farm was the focal point for the family and friends on weekends, and especially holidays. It was a popular place for homemade ice cream on Sunday afternoons, both summer and winter.

The ice cream maker was a large pail about 28 inches tall with a lid and crank that clamped onto the pail. A round container held the custard to be frozen into ice cream and was placed inside the pail with a space between the container and the pail. Just plain ice would not freeze the cream, and it needed rock salt to make the ice cold enough. The salted ice was put in to surround the container in the space between the container and the pail. The container had gears on top that the crank clamped onto to turn the container.

Mom cooked the custard for the ice cream, and whoever was there took turns cranking the freezer. If the salted ice melted, it had to be replaced until the cream was frozen. When it was too hard to turn the crank, that meant the ice cream was frozen and ready to eat. Excitement all around! To keep it (since we had no electricity), the container had to be banked with ice and rock salt and covered with a heavy blanket. We used a horse blanket to keep it cold.

This was all done in the shed. Dad would bring in a cake of ice from the stack and chip enough ice off with an axe, and what wasn't used was put in the milk cooler. In the summer, we made at least two freezers-full, about two gallons, of ice cream each time. We usually had two kinds, vanilla and chocolate, and when the wild strawberries were ripe at the Hathorn place, I (sometimes with Ruth) would pick enough for one freezer of ice cream.

Thanksgiving was a day off for everyone, but it was also a hunting day, so dinner didn't start until late afternoon when we were all back from hunting. George and Betty and their family were there. Betty helped with the cooking. My grandmother and her husband. Harold and Mary and their kids came late because they lived with Mary's family and had dinner with them. Our dining table had three leaves and there was room for everyone.

There weren't any wild turkeys around then, so we didn't have turkey for Thanksgiving, we had goose. Mom raised geese to sell at Thanksgiving and Christmas, so we had one of them. Also chicken and roast deer meat, mashed potatoes, squash, green beans, cranberry sauce, mincemeat pie (from deer mincemeat I'd ground), and apple pie from our apples.

At Christmas, there was usually snow, so we'd put on snowshoes to go up over the hill the week before to find our tree, and drag a sled for the tree. We'd find a pretty good one right off but think there'd be an even better one further on, and then a better one beyond that. In the end, we'd come back to the first one.

Christmas dinner was always a brunch at home, and everyone would come for the brunch and then presents under the tree. Mom's presents for us and for the grandkids were usually things she'd knitted, mittens or socks or scarves or sweaters.

Other times of the year, people would just show up on the weekend, Mom and Dad's friends, my friends, neighbors and kin. Mom would insist they stay, and she'd feed them, which she liked doing. In the summer, homemade ice cream; in the winter, pancakes or waffles and our maple syrup.

My parents and their friends had a good time together. They'd visit each other's houses, sometimes play cards in teams against each other. There would be small prizes for the winners, and always "refreshments" and homemade dessert. There'd be other games, like checkers, which Dad loved playing. He seldom lost. After Carroll and Susie got TV, we would visit and watch boxing or wrestling. I'd usually curl up and go to sleep.

Dad tried not to do major work on Sundays, but if we'd had a lot of rain and there was sunshine, it had to be done.

On a good Sunday, we'd go down to the ocean, Pemaquid Point or Popham Beach, especially if there'd been a storm and we could watch the surf. In those days, there were places along the river or the ocean-front (in Georgetown or Five Islands, or Small's Point in Phippsburg) where people could picnic undisturbed, and build fires. We'd bring cooked lobsters, build a fire, and steam clams. Sometimes George Jr. and his family would go with us.

After Harold and George Jr. were married and out of the house, they'd sometimes treat Dad to a weekend at Moosehead Lake fishing for landlocked salmon and togue. Ruth and Jud would come stay at the farm to help do chores and milk the cows.

Everyone's social life changed with the introduction of TV. You didn't have to go out and see people for entertainment. Entertainment came to you, right there in a big box in your own house. Friday night was cards night with Carroll and Susie, and that continued, sometimes with Jud and Ruth, who used to eat supper with us on Fridays. Dad would pick Ruth up during the day, and Jud would come after work. Some Friday nights at Carroll and Susie's, they just watched the fights. Since electricity didn't come to our house before the 1950s, we didn't have TV until then either, or a telephone. The Allens had a telephone, and they were good about getting messages to us.

My brothers and Ruth got together and bought Mom and Dad a TV set and a huge antenna that they installed on the roof. The antenna had a motor so you could turn it in order to get the best reception. We could get Portland and Mt. Washington, and usually Bangor, but Bangor might have some "snow." Sometimes you could get Boston and see a Red Sox game, but that was almost always through a lot of snow.

CHAPTER TWENTY

The Last Chapter

The Ames farm was the backbone of five generations of our Ames family. Dad loved everything about it. He didn't have a great education, but he learned by watching and by doing. He knew what was important, how to maintain and manage a herd of cows for their milk, hens for their eggs and for food, how to tend to the horses, to work the land, to raise crops for his family and to sell, and how to preserve and maintain the farm so it could be passed on to the next generation. Just as his great-great-grandfather Jacob Eames had done 150 years earlier, and every Eames and Ames who succeeded Jacob had done.

Love stories are supposed to have a happy ending, but this is not one of those. There were many reasons.

There was an economic boom after World War II. Good-paying jobs without the rigors of the farm were available for young men who were married and raising families, as my three brothers were. Taking up subsistence farming again was not an attractive proposition for them.

It never had been for Harold. Not long after completing the training and apprenticeship programs, he hired on as a machinist at Bath Iron Works. He would work at BIW for 42 years as a master machinist, most of those years on the four to midnight shift. (Harold liked that shift because it gave him the daylight hours to do what he wanted, including taking his wife, Mary, to her job at an oil company office in Bath.)

He and Mary, who was raised on Prince Edward Island, married in 1938 and stayed on the farm in the "other part" for a short time, until they found an apartment to rent in Bath. They had two children, a son, Harold Jr., who would become a BIW "lifer" like his dad, as a master welder; and a daughter, Judy. They rented in Bath for 20 years until Mary's parents came down from P.E.I., moved in with them, and bought the house they were renting.

Harold, the oldest, would have been Dad's logical successor, but he didn't like the farm and wasn't interested in it. Dad had raised him, as he raised all of us, to be independent, and Harold was. If there was a job to be done on the farm where Dad needed his help, like shingling, he would come help. Otherwise, we would never see him or his family unless he came hunting with a friend, or at holidays.

Gilbert liked the family and the farm well enough—he was one of our best hunters, and I will never forget his flying back from California to take me to my senior dance—but he had reasons not to come back, even though he had worked at Hyde Windlass before he enlisted in the war. He was married to a local girl then, in 1942, but she couldn't wait for the war to end and so divorced him. That was hard.

After he was discharged in September 1945, he came home briefly, but he liked Southern California—he had trained as a pilot at Edwards Air Force Base, and he had met out there the woman who would become his second wife—another Mary (known in the family as "Marie," to distinguish her from Harold's wife) who wanted to stay and live there. She had a daughter from a prior marriage, and she and Gil would have another daughter together.

Gil wanted to continue to fly, and he had found himself a job in the Edwards tool shop, where he would eventually be known as "the last manual toolmaker" (before the computers took over) and which he would eventually run for over twenty years. He had a good heart, and spent most of his spare time helping people who didn't have much, providing them with used clothing and much-needed foodstuffs. And he could keep on flying.

Gil and I continued to be close. He would buy the tickets or send me the airfare, and I would go to California to visit every year or so. He and Marie were married for thirty years, until she died of cancer. He was lonesome and said I should come to California, but I had responsibilities, including that Dad was living with me. Gil remarried, but it was not the happiest marriage. He developed heart problems, like Mom, and died at 72.

George had also wanted to be a pilot, and the Air Force sent him to Alabama, to Birmingham Southern College, for pilot training. He couldn't pass the pilots' eye exam, so they made him a tail gunner on a B-17 at the age of 18 (go figure). He met his wife, Mary, at Birmingham Southern (she was a freshman there).

They married a week after his discharge, were married for 54 years, and raised three children, George III, Mary Elizabeth, and Barbara Ann, before he died from cancer.

All my brothers married a Mary. George's Mary was Mary Elizabeth, so we called her "Betty." Betty was really something, a southern girl who didn't mind the cold. Dad used to tell her he wouldn't take her outside with him unless she put some clothes on.

After they were first married, George and Betty lived in the "other part" for two or three years. I was still in high school, and both George and I helped with the chores on the farm. George also helped Dad on his work as Road Commissioner, and Betty kept busy helping Mom, and having kids. Betty had their two oldest children when they were living in the "other," and was pregnant with Barbara Ann when they moved. A lot of noise and a lot of laundry.

George had bought a truck and was hiring out on his own when he got a job at BIW, and he and Betty moved to Sagadahoc, where they would raise their family. I stayed with them there when I was going to high school in Bath. They and their kids spent a lot of time on the farm—the kids practically grew up there, and they loved it.

George worked at BIW for 18 years in the maintenance department, but hated the work because it kept him inside all the time. He wanted to be outside, so he bought a dragger and went deep sea fishing off the coast south of Sebasco Estates. His son, George III, was working for Cianbro at the time and took a leave from his job to help his dad get started. One day in January, as they were docking, he slipped, fell overboard, hit his head, and drowned. George III was only 22. I like to think that he would have wanted to take over the farm if he could, but he never had the chance, and we'll never know.

George never recovered emotionally from the loss of his son, but after a while, he went back out fishing again, and continued fishing for quite a few years until his hands became so affected by arthritis he couldn't handle the nets. He always thought of fishing as farming of the sea.

Ruth and Jud, who had married in 1935, never lived in the "other part" and had made their life in Bath, but they didn't have children. They were both very good in helping out at the farm in their spare time, Jud especially. Whenever a spare hand was needed, Jud was there, and when my brothers took Dad to Moosehead for a weekend fishing, Jud and Ruth would move in, and Jud and I would do the chores while Ruth helped Mom.

Jud worked at Hyde Windlass for more than 30 years in the "tool crib," where he maintained the tools used in Hyde's manufacturing. Ruth worked in the cutting room of Congress Sportswear in Bath. Ruth's job would have tragic results after she developed a persistent cough from the lint in the cutting room, and her doctor prescribed a codeine-based cough medicine. She became addicted.

It was tragic for all of us, but especially for Mom and Dad, who had to watch their oldest child deteriorate. She spent nine months in recovery at a facility in upstate Massachusetts. She was never the same, and her treatment had an effect on her memory. Jud died of cancer, and after that she just gave up. She died at 67, not long after Mom and Dad had both passed.

Even closer to home, Mom had had a severe case of rheumatic fever in 1945 and was in bed for six weeks. It got really bad before it was diagnosed. Ruth came and stayed during the week and I took care of her weekends. I was 13. The doctor was really concerned about her then, and said my brothers should come see her. George was in Italy but Gilbert got home. The episode left her heart compromised. She wasn't able to do as much as she did before, so Ruth and I helped as much as we could.

I had thought Mom and Dad were indefatigable. I never understood how she could do all the things she did. Dad never even had a cold. When he thought one might be coming on, he cured it with a slug of rum from the bottle he kept up over the kitchen cupboard. To me, they seemed invincible. But they weren't. Not even Dad.

When Mom had the rheumatic fever, we didn't know how bad it was, or how badly it affected her (she would never talk about stuff). It was hard for her to get the energy to get out of bed in the morning. So the first part of cooking I took over was breakfast. I did the chores with Dad, but had to leave him in the barn before they were done to go make breakfast, and then get off to school. Ruth would come out after work to help with dinner. Between Ruth and me, we did most of the cooking.

I took over all of it as a teenager.

I stayed at the farm after graduating from Morse High, did the chores with Dad—couldn't leave him to do it all himself—and helped out with Mom. In 1953, I married Victor, and we moved into the "other part" for three or four years. Vic worked at the First National in Damariscotta as a meat cutter and later managed its meat department, but he didn't drive, so I drove him every day, and picked him up again. That got old, and we moved to Nobleboro in 1957, close to the First National, although we spent summers at the cottage on the farm where my grandmother had lived. Vic loved the farm, and between us and with my brother George's considerable help, Dad was able to keep the dairy farm going. But not without costs.

He became more and more anxious as he saw the life he had always known sliding away from him. With the coming of electricity and television, whatever their benefits, the rhythm of life he and Mom had known was changed forever. Instead of exchanging visits and socializing with relatives, neighbors, and friends, people could get their enjoyment and entertainment from the TV. Instead of listening to the radio, which you could do while you were doing other things, you had to watch the TV. People just didn't get together anymore the way they used to.

> The State passed Milk Control laws in 1935 and created the Maine Milk Commission to oversee the milk industry, to "support the viability" of farms and set minimum prices for milk so that "there will be a plentiful supply of pure, wholesome milk." You'd think that would have helped the small farmer, but it didn't work that way.

We were a small dairy farm. We weren't in dairy farming as a business, but to feed, clothe, and take care of the family, and to provide some money we could spend. There used to be a lot of small dairy farms like us, and it all worked until the State took over managing the milk industry. Then, little by little, it all went wrong for us and the other small farmers because the State favored the big milk producers and didn't care for—or do anything to help or take care of—the small farmers.

Dad was bitter about it and called it "the big fish eating the small fish."

We were able at first to keep up with the small changes, like the change in size of the milk cans from 8 gallons to 12 gallons, although Dad had to rig up the pulley system to handle the bigger cans. There was no extra money to buy equipment to make our work easier, so we had to work harder to get the job done.

And we were able to meet the sanitary requirements. Uncle Dave and Aunt Annie were able to afford to buy pasteurizing equipment, so they sold direct to their customers and not to a dairy. We couldn't afford to buy the equipment, but we were selling to Oakhurst, who took care of the pasteurizing, so that was okay for a while. The problem we had with Oakhurst was Dad didn't trust them to be honest in testing our milk for butterfat content and weighing it.

> We got paid by both weight and butterfat content—two different prices—and when I started driving our milk cans, Dad told me to stand beside the Oakhurst employee to watch and protect the readings on both. That way, we knew we were getting paid what we were due.

Our efforts to meet what the State and Oakhurst required of us all ended around 1960 when the State required all dairy farmers to buy 100-gallon bulk milk tanks so Oakhurst could come in with their tanker trucks to siphon up our milk out of the bulk tank. We couldn't deliver our milk in milk cans anymore, and we'd have to figure out how to clean the bulk tank. It was fine with Oakhurst because they had been getting bigger and bigger, were buying up smaller dairies, and were only interested in buying milk from big production dairy farms. Even though being able to have their tankers pick up milk from bulk milk tanks was something that benefited them, they were not going to help the small farmer with the cost of the tanks or cleaning them.

Not only that, but Dad would have had to expand the farm and buy more cows to be able to fill the tank. The tank by itself would have been a $10,000 investment. Dad was 68 years old, and he knew he couldn't regain the money he would have to borrow. He couldn't stay in the dairy farm business and had no choice but to sell his beloved herd.

Dad was unable to cope, emotionally, with the loss of his herd, which he'd worked so hard to build up and to nurture into a productive dairy farm, and with the fact that none of his children were willing, for one reason or another, to shoulder the burden of continuing the work needed to maintain the farm. It got so bad he had to be hospitalized for depression and given shock treatments, which wiped away the depression, but also a large part of his memory. He had to be told it was time for him to get back to work. Which he did. He busied himself cutting wood and doing maintenance on the buildings.

The government had just begun Social Security for self-employed people, so his accountant helped him get as much Social Security as he could. It wasn't much, but my grandmother had left my mother what she had accrued from her three husbands, and that was what they had to live on. They left the farm on December 1, 1965, to spend the winter with my second husband, George, and me at our house. They intended to go back to the farm in the spring, but they never did.

When I was little, with Ruth and my brothers having left the farm, I was alone a lot, lonely, and I would ask my Mom why I'd been born. She would smile and say, "God gave you to us for a reason…"

Dad got sick in the spring. We were told he had cancer of the lung, and he was in and out of the hospital most of the summer. It was hard on me because I was working two jobs and went to the hospital almost every night to see him. Through more X-rays, they found his lung clear but he wouldn't believe them.

I was worn thin by then and passed out one day and got a concussion. Dad decided I needed his help, which got him on his feet again.

Then my Mom's sister Irene's husband died suddenly and she came to live with us—and there were five of us in a five-room house for about three months. On Christmas night, Mom had a heart attack and died. What a year that was!

Dad never went back to the farm to live, and it was traumatic for him to sell it. He stayed on with us until he died in 1980.

Dad was unhappy about the fact that he couldn't pass the farm down to another generation. The fact that it had been in our family for five generations was important to him. He used to say, "I have to get over it." In his will, he left the back pasture (which he'd kept out of the sale of the farm) to Harold Jr. so that someone in the Ames family would still own a part of the Ames Farm.

John and Eleanore Thorpe, who he sold the farm to in 1968, were a retired couple who saw our farm as a beautiful place where they could garden, raise some vegetables, and enjoy living by the river. They were not farmers. John was a pastor, but without a church. They were both kind people, and Dad and Ellie hit it off. Whenever they were thinking about changing something, she'd call Dad and invite him to come talk about it. For that matter, they invited him to come visit whenever he felt like it, and he did. I would drive him there.

He had a place in the kitchen where he liked to sit, and where he could look out to the barn and the milk shed, and where the ice stack had been, and over the fields where he had made his life planting, harvesting, and working with his herd. I can still see him sitting there, looking out and thinking for long periods.

Don't even need to close my eyes.

Afterword and History of the Ames Farm

<hr/>

I am grateful to Roberta for her memoir of life on the Farm. In the course of working with her on this book, I researched the history of ownership of the property and describe it below. The ownership and its history may be of interest because of the light it sheds on pre-Colonial, Colonial, and American history, including ownership disputes over land in that part of Maine which includes the Farm, among the Kennebec Proprietors, the Clarke and Lake Company, and Abenaki Native Americans, and the close relationship between England's Massachusetts Bay Colony and its Province of Maine before the Revolution, and well before the latter became a state.

Jacob Eames (the spelling of the name changed later) was the first recorded owner of the Farm at age 23, having received a deed to its original 100 acres in 1779 from John Winn, a prominent member of the community of Wilmington, Massachusetts, for a consideration of £350. Jacob and four generations of his descendants would own and work the land and its farm for nearly 200 years, into the 1960s.

The progenitor of the family that would eventually include George Ames and his daughter Roberta, the author of this memoir, was Jacob's great-grandfather Samuel Eames (1664–1747), also of Wilmington. Jacob's grandfather, Daniel Eames (1697–1781), was the third of Samuel's eleven children, and his father—also named Jacob—was the fifth of Daniel's six children. Jacob himself was born in 1756, the oldest of his father's ten children. (Interestingly, both Jacobs would marry wives named Lucy. Lucy Frost was Jacob's mother, and Lucy Jones, whom he would marry in 1780, his wife.)

Daniel Eames was a Captain in Wilmington's militia, duly appointed by King George II, and a veteran of the French and Indian War (1756–1763). He and another prominent citizen of Wilmington,

Cadwallader Ford, who had fought alongside Daniel in the war and was likewise a captain in the Wilmington militia, would later join forces to acquire land in Maine.

The issues concerning ownership of land in Maine in the first half of the 1700s were difficult. Maine was an unsettled frontier owned by the King—or perhaps by the Massachusetts Bay Colony—or perhaps by the Native Americans (referred to as "Indians" in the usage of the times). The King had granted land; the Colony had granted land; the Native American tribes had signed deeds to land; and the description of the land in all those cases was inexact.

No one had effectively mapped this area of Maine, and the creation of a "map" was generally commissioned by one side or the other in a land dispute, based on its own favorable interpretation of the language in a land grant or deed. Disputes were numerous.

The Woolwich area was at the center of one of those disputes, and the dispute included ownership of the land that was to become the Ames Farm.

In the mid-1750s, the ownership of the land bordering the Kennebec River from north of Woolwich south to the Atlantic, was disputed among Native Americans, the Kennebec Proprietors (mostly Boston-based land speculators), and the Clarke and Lake Company, founded by two officers for the Crown, Major Thomas Clarke and Captain Thomas Lake, who had distinguished themselves in King Phillip's War (1675–1678) and been rewarded with land grants in Maine. Even before that war, they had been the recipients of Native American tribes' deeds to the lower Kennebec River area (an old map, no doubt commissioned by them, refers to their purchases of 1649 and 1653), and had established, in 1654, a trading post and settlement in Arrowsic. Natives attacked and destroyed it in 1676, killing 30 settlers, including Lake. Clarke died of natural causes in 1683, but the company's interests and claims continued in the hands of the company's investors.

The Kennebec Proprietors claimed most of the land on both sides of the lower Kennebec River down to the Atlantic, including the land claimed by Clarke and Lake, under a purchase from the Massachusetts Bay Colony. The Proprietors asserted dominion over their claim in various ways, including by commissioning maps that laid out lots, and by granting those lots to individuals. One of the original Proprietors, Nathaniel Thwing Sr., had acquired two lots of 100 acres each in Woolwich in 1726, one of which included what is now Thwings Point, jutting into the Kennebec River adjacent to and south of the later Ames Farm. He began construction of a house there in 1754. (Woolwich History, p. 248)

When the land ownership dispute between the Proprietors and the Clarke and Lake interests arose in the 1750s, the spokesman for the Clarke and Lake interests was Cadwallader Ford of Wilmington, who was listed as "Clerk, Treasurer and strategist." The outcome of the litigation, as the result of a hearing and referees' report, was to award to the Clarke and Lake interests in 1757 the land comprising the town of Woolwich, Arrowsic Island (just below Woolwich), and 350 acres on Parker's Island. More disputes and legal maneuvering by the Proprietors followed, until the parties agreed to a settlement under which, for a payment of £450 by the Proprietors, the report was accepted, and Clarke and Lake released to the Proprietors all the land north of the Woolwich line. (Kershaw, *The Kennebec Proprietors, 1749–1775*, pp. 154–158)

As reported by Robert H. Gardiner, one of the Proprietors, in describing four land disputes with which the Proprietors dealt:

> The controversy with Clarke and Lake was the first settled. They claimed under Indian deeds, and after sundry lawsuits and references, it was decided in 1758, that on the east side of Kennebec river, the north line of the present town of Woolwich should be the south boundary of the Plymouth Patent, and the north line of Clarke and Lake. (*History of the Kennebec Purchase*, vol. II, pp. 276–277, by R.H. Gardiner, Esq.; Maine Historical Society Collection)

Thus, despite the Proprietors' claim to it, the land which was to become the Ames Farm, located just to the south of the north line of

Woolwich, was determined to be the property of Clarke and Lake.

Having led Clarke and Lake to their victory over the Proprietors, Cadwallader Ford sought to acquire further land in Maine, this time in association with his friend and soldier-in-arms Daniel Eames. Soldiers who had fought in the French and Indian War had been paid in the form of "scrip" issued by the Massachusetts Bay Colony ("scrip" was essentially an IOU for later payment), and the two of them set about buying as much of the scrip as they could, which the Colony then redeemed in exchange for tracts of land in Maine. This scheme was regarded by some as questionable, even nefarious, and led to the writing of a letter, now in the Massachusetts State Archives, calling them "a royal pair of rascals." (August 17, 2019 *Wilmington Town Crier*)

It is impossible today to piece together the connections between the Wilmington neighbors Daniel Eames, Cadwallader Ford, and John Winn, their interests in Clarke and Lake, the impact of the Clarke and Lake settlement with the Proprietors, the acquisition and redemption of soldiers' scrip for Maine land, and the purchase of the Ames Farm 20 years after the Clarke and Lake/Proprietors settlement by Daniel Eames's young grandson Jacob. It is tempting to speculate, even 250 years later: It seems unlikely that Jacob himself, at 23, had the wherewithal for the purchase price. Was it a wedding gift in anticipation of Jacob's forthcoming marriage to Lucy Jones? What persuaded Jacob and Lucy to move to Maine for their new life together? It seems likely that these events and relationships played a role.

John Winn's deed (see Appendix) describes the land conveyed as follows:

> "[A] certain Tract of Land lying in Woolwich in the County of Lincoln and Province aforesaid, containing by my Estimation one Hundred Acres and is bounded westerly on Merrymeeting Bay, Southerly on the Land of Nathaniel Thwing, Esq., Easterly on the line of One Thousand Acre Lot granted and laid out by [the] Prop[rietors] holding under Clarke and Lake to William Skinner, deceased, the said Hundred Acres is to extend Northerly from the said Thwing's Line until said Hundred Acres be compleated…

When Jacob acquired the hundred-acre Ames Farm in 1779, his neighbor to the south, on what is now called Thwings Point, was Nathaniel Thwing Jr., son of one of one of the original Kennebec Proprietors. His father had acquired his claim to the property more than 30 years before the litigation with Clarke and Lake, and had built a home on it. Although the litigation and its settlement had invalidated the Proprietors' claims on the land, no one—and certainly not Clarke and Lake, who were seeking settlers for the land they now owned—was going to dispute the Thwings' title to the land and the home they had built.

Jacob Eames, 24 years old, married Lucy Jones, 21, in 1780. Over the next 27 years, 18 of which were spent building a home on, and turning the hundred-acre Winn purchase in Woolwich into a working farm, they had five children, of whom the third, David Jaquith Eames (1800–1864), was the oldest son and would succeed to the ownership of the farm upon Jacob's death in 1839. (He also changed the spelling of the family name to Ames because no one could pronounce Eames correctly.) He married Elizabeth Farnham, with whom he had nine children, including Gilbert Jacob Ames (1824–1876), the oldest, who would in turn succeed to the ownership of the farm. Gilbert had six children, including David Jacob Ames (1867–1903), Roberta's grandfather.

Gilbert Ames and his son, David Jacob Ames, owned and ran the Ames Farm during the heyday of the Kennebec River ice-harvesting industry in the mid to late 1800s. While there are no records of the Ames families' involvement in the industry, it is inconceivable that they were not employed in it every winter, as was every farmer along the Kennebec looking for work during idle winter hours—and for ready cash for their labors. The Morse Ice Co. of Bath had built, on Thwings Point, three icehouses with a storage capacity of 75,000 tons, the greatest capacity of any icehouse location on the Kennebec River, and the Ames families possessed (and still possessed in Roberta's time) the tools of the trade, including the saws needed to cut the ice (which George Ames would later use to supply his own icehouse).

It also seems likely that the Ames Farm provided room and board for some of the workers.

> There were three sets of [icehouses on Thwings Point]. In addition to ice houses, boarding houses nearby were needed for the crews. Neighboring farmers' wives often took some of the ice crew to board for additional income. (*History of Woolwich, Maine*, p. 141)

David Ames had two children, George and Ann, four years George's senior. David died a tragic death by drowning in the river when his son George was 12. George then had to leave school to help his mother and older sister run the farm. Ann married David Henderson in 1909, and the two of them ran Henderson's Dairy Farm in Bath.

George Ames lived and worked on the Ames Farm, and ran it, for over 70 years. Over that period, self-educated from the age of 12, he provided for his wife, Ida, and their family of five children, born over 16 years during the height of the Great Depression, as he slowly acquired the cattle needed for a dairy farm. As Roberta has described it, life on the Farm was both difficult and rewarding. It was what George Ames knew, his life.

In the 1960s, the Ames Farm was, as it had been for 40 years, largely a dairy farm. George Ames was 70, his three sons had no interest in taking over from him, and the regulations imposed on dairy farming by the State of Maine had made its dairy operations virtually impossible for him, even with the help of his youngest child, Roberta, and her husband, and occasional help from two of his three sons. He had to sell the cows and the bull, something that pained him badly—it was the end of the life he had led for 60 years, the last of the Ames family to own and run the farm. And then he had to sell the farm itself, his family's heritage for nearly 200 years.

Erik Lund
Woolwich, Maine
June 2021

Know all Men by these Presents, That I John Winn of Willmington in the County of said Middlesex and Province of Massachusetts Bay in New England, Yeoman, in Consideration of the Sum of three hundred and fifty Pounds lawful Money paid me by Jacob Eames of Willmington in the County and Province aforesaid, Yeoman; The Receipt whereof I do hereby acknowledge, do hereby give, grant, sell and convey unto the said Jacob Eames, his Heirs and Assigns, one certain Tract of Land lying in Woolwich in the County of Lincoln and Province aforesaid, containing by by Estimation one Hundred Acres, and is bounded Westerly on Merremeten Bay, Southerly on the Land of Nathaniel Thwing Esq.ᵣ, Easterly on the Line of one Thousand Acre lot granted and laid out by the Prop.ʳˢ holding under Clarke and Lake to William Skinner Esq.ʳ deceas'd, the said hundred Acres is to ex_

Deed from John Winn to Jacob Eames, dated March 15, 1779.

-tend Northerly from the said Thwing's Line until said Hundred Acres be compleated, excepting the Road laid out across said Hundred Acres, and to extend twelve Rods further North by the Land granted to Skinner aforesaid, then it is to extend Northward on Merrymeeting Bay that is it is to be twelve Rods wider on the Easterly End than it is on the Westerly End thus as it is bounded.

To have and to hold the same to the said Jacob Eames, his Heirs and Assigns, to his and their Use and Behoof forever. And I do covenant with the said Jacob Eames, his Heirs and Assigns, That I am lawfully seized in Fee of the Premises; that they are free of all Incumbrances, That I have good Right to sell and convey the same to the said Jacob Eames, and that I will warrant and defend the same to the said Jacob Eames, his Heirs and Assigns forever, against the lawful Claims and Demands of all Persons. In Witness whereof I have hereunto set my Hand and Seal this fifteenth Day of March Anno Domini

1779. Signed, sealed and deliver'd in Presence of us. — John Winn & a Seal — Joshua Harnden John Going. — Middlesex ss. March 30. 1779. — John Winn above named acknowledged the above Instrument to his Deed. — Coram Josiah Johnson Just. Pace. — Lincoln ss. Received April 19. 1779, and accordingly entered and examined

by Jona. Bowman Regr

87.

About Roberta Ames and Erik Lund

———————⋗●⋖———————

Roberta Ames is a member of the sixth generation of the Ames family to live on the Ames Farm in Woolwich, Maine, and is the last member of the family to have been born and raised there.

Despite the hardships—the farm had no electricity, no running water, no ice other than what was harvested from the river, and the family's workday began every day, summer or winter, at 4:30 a.m.—she loved the farm and all the attributes of a subsistence farming family's life. It was a personal tragedy for her, as well as for her father and mother, when circumstances made it clear they could no longer maintain the farm, and the farm had to pass out of the Ames family after nearly 200 years.

In this memoir, Roberta recounts the farming life in which she was raised in the 1930s, 1940s, and 1950s, not for nostalgia's sake alone, but to document that way of life before it is forgotten forever. Although the Ames family raised crops for themselves and for sale, their farm was primarily a dairy farm with a herd of twenty-five cows, calves, and heifers, which had to be tended to every day.

Roberta Ames was born in 1931, the youngest of five children of George and Ida Ames, who were then 39 and 38, respectively. She lived and worked on the Ames Farm until she was 26, the last five of those years together with her husband, Victor. When he was transferred by his employer, they had no choice but to leave the farm. Her siblings did not want to take over the farm, and the herd was sold in 1961. Her parents stayed on, doing maintenance and other chores until 1965, when they, too, had to leave, and moved in with Roberta and her husband. The farm was later sold.

Roberta was employed in a variety of capacities until 1972, when she became an administrator in the Lincoln County Sheriff's office in

Wiscasset, and resumed her education at the University of Maine in Augusta. There, she took evening courses until she graduated in 1975 with an Associate's Degree in Criminal Justice. Having since retired, she makes her home in Nobleboro, Maine.

Erik Lund was raised in Augusta, Maine, where he graduated from Cony High School. He later attended and graduated from Bowdoin College and Harvard Law School. Having retired from the practice of law, he and his wife, Sandy, live in Woolwich, Maine, on a portion of what was once the Ames Farm.

Special Acknowledgment

Although we did this book together, I want to thank Erik specially because it would never have happened without him. He knew what questions to ask to draw out my memories, and then he knew how to put them all together. We had fun doing it, but it was work, too. I will be forever grateful for everything he did to make this book possible.

Roberta Ames
June 2021

Acknowledgments

As with every book, even one as small as this one, many other people contributed to it, and the book would not have been possible without their help. Primary among them have been Richard Geldard and Ruth Koury. Richard, a distinguished author as well as a Bowdoin classmate and fraternity brother of Erik's, read and critiqued chapter after chapter as we worked on them. Ruth, Erik's assistant from his time at Posternak, Blankstein & Lund, patiently recorded drafts of the chapters and their many changes and edits, suggested design, and added her comments as we went along.

Genie Dailey and Lindy Gifford edited and designed the book for publication, and Lindy willingly took on many related tasks on which we would not have been competent. Bill Bunting, Jennifer Bunting, Stephen Cole, Ginny Cunningham, Susan and David Gay, Jon Lund, Joan Sturmthal, and Janet Yost have read drafts of the book and given helpful comments and suggestions.

We are grateful to all of them because without them, Roberta's dream of publishing a memoir of her family's life on their farm in Woolwich would not have been fulfilled. Thank you all from both of us.

Roberta Ames
Erik Lund
June 2021

CPSIA information can be obtained
at www.ICGtesting.com
Printed in the USA
BVHW071409091221
623633BV00005B/156